MEXICO CITY

MEXICO CITY

AN OPINIONATED GUIDE FOR THE CURIOUS TRAVELER
BY
JIM JOHNSTON
PHOTOGRAPHS BY NICHOLAS GILMAN

iUniverse, Inc.
New York Lincoln Shanghai

Mexico City
An Opinionated Guide for the Curious Traveler

Copyright © 2006 by James Patrick Johnston

iUniverse books may be ordered through booksellers or by contacting:

iUniverse
2021 Pine Lake Road, Suite 100
Lincoln, NE 68512
www.iuniverse.com
1-800-Authors (1-800-288-4677)

Design and Cover Design: Nicholas Gilman

ISBN-13: 978-0-595-41841-1 (pbk)
ISBN-13: 978-0-595-86183-5 (ebk)
ISBN-10: 0-595-41841-4 (pbk)
ISBN-10: 0-595-86183-0 (ebk)

Printed in the United States of America

I would like to thank Daniel Barrón, Harriet & Irving Berg, Valeria Clark, Tony Cohan, Beverly Donofrio, Janice Eidus, Luisa Field, Pauline Frommer, Regina Gómez & Angel Valtierra, Romney Lang, Barbara Luboff, Jaime Montes, Dolores Quintera, Carol Romano, Luis and Elodie Santamaria, Masako Takahashi, Rachel Wysoker and Nicholas Gilman for their invaluable assistance in creating this book.

CONTENTS

INTRODUCTION

When I tell people I live in Mexico City, the response is often bewilderment shadowed with trepidation. As one of the biggest conglomerations of human beings on the planet, its sheer size can be daunting, and everybody (especially those who have never been here) has a crime or a pollution story, the grittier the better. But as a resident explorer of the city for more than 10 years, I have come to know it well, to manage its complexities, to make it enjoyable, even delectable. What started out as a collection of notes on my discoveries around town to share with friends has grown into this guidebook, a love letter to my home town, known here simply as *Mexico* or *el DF* (el day-effay), *el Distrito Federal*. It is a biased book, I admit, rooted in a love that accepts many imperfections, without overlooking them. I include a number of popular tourist sites that nobody should miss, but also lesser-known places, neighborhoods, markets, and even a specific street corner where you will find the best tamales. My opinions are colored by my professional life as an artist and architect, and by my interest in good food.

Mexico City isn't really beautiful like Paris or San Francisco—its gems lie in a matrix of urban hysteria. It can delight and assault the senses with equal force, and teasingly hide much of its allure behind massive old walls. With population estimates as high as 25 million, the tumult of noise and activity can be overwhelming, and the extremes of wealth and poverty can be unsettling. There is a great deal of sensory input here, and it takes some effort to sort it all out. Unlike more demure European or American cities, Mexico pours out onto its streets with unrestrained exuberance. Color is everywhere: radiant magenta, acidic lime green, or screeching yellow will suddenly appear on a wall or a shirt, a balloon or a piece of fruit. Advertising is boldly painted directly on building walls, creating a delightful, if disorienting, overabundance of visual information. With zoning laws often ignored, startling juxtapositions occur, and you might see a stately colonial building next to a 60's-style gas station. Hand-hewn stones, irregular surfaces, and cobbled streets create a softer physical texture than many modern cities. Except for some of the newer, wealthy areas, the slick, cold feel of steel, glass and industrial precision is minimal.

Mexico City has a great sound track, and I often stop and listen. Organ grinders play throughout the city, an old tradition which arrived with Italian immigrants a century ago (give a tip—it's their only source of income); singers accompany themselves with guitars and accordions in the streets, in restaurants and in the metro. Market vendors have their particular calls and cadences (called *pregones*), knife sharpeners have their distinctive whistle (not to be confused with the whistle of the *camotero* who sells cooked sweet potatoes in the evening) and even the garbage collectors have a particular sound, the clanging of a metal bell, to announce their arrival. There is a hum of constant traffic, but the jolting blare of honking horns, car alarms and sirens is surprisingly uncommon, and the noise of jackhammers almost nonexistent—quieter sounds of manual labor generally prevail, even on large construction sites. Volume and cacophony are more often experienced as pleasure than annoyance by Mexicans—visit Plaza Garibaldi one night to hear the mariachis and you will know what I mean.

The city smells of life in ways you don't find in more sanitized places. Open food stalls are everywhere: a pervasive aroma of corn tortillas, roasting meats, chiles, and *garapiñados* (nuts cooked in caramelized sugar) are just a few of the pleasurable smells that mix with the noxious exhaust of too many vehicles. Air quality has been steadily improving over the past few years, however, and there are many days with clear blue skies.

Mexico City has a bit of an old-fashioned feel, comfortable in its long cultural heritage, not terribly concerned with trends or fads. Old style barbershops, wooden-door cantinas, dowdy ladies' corset shops, and glass-bottle pharmacies are found throughout the city, some of them untouched for 50 years or more. Modern Mexico City also has plenty of slick, high-rise stuff, and lots of super-rich people living behind walls, mostly in the western suburbs. Chic hotels, elegant restaurants and designer stores are here, but they tend to have the same feeling as elsewhere, so I don't include too much of that in my book. A deep sense of ancient history pervades the city as well. The faces of many people, the food, and place names such as Chapultepec, Popocatepetl and Nezahuacoyatl reflect its Aztec past. A sense of the world not changing, an embrace of history, is what gives this city its special character, but with the forces of globalization pounding at the gates, I don't think it will last much longer. It's a good time to visit.

Mexico City is not for the faint-hearted traveler. The air is polluted, the traffic is beyond belief, it's in an earthquake zone, and within range of a smoking volcano. You don't come to relax or "get away from it all." You come to be seduced by a flourishing 700-year old culture, by people whose hearts are easily opened, and by the sheer audacity of it all. Keep your senses alert to the stimuli and you will be richly rewarded. I hope this book will help enable you to discover Mexico City and to love it as I do.

Street artists in el Tepito

TRAVEL TIPS

PLANNING/ ARRIVAL/
GETTING AROUND/
HELPFUL HINTS

When to Visit There is no really bad time to visit Mexico City—the climate is as close to year-round springtime as you will find anywhere. My favorite month is March when the jacaranda trees are in full bloom—the huge clouds of lavender blossoms are a stunning sight. April and May can be hot and dry, December and January can be chilly at night and the rainy season (late May through October) can bring some days of London-like gloom, but in general Mexico is not a country with extremes of climate, and a week without sunshine is rare. The city is quiet between Christmas and New Year, but comes alive immediately afterwards for *Dia de los Tres Magos* (January 6). *Semana Santa* (the week before Easter) is another quiet time, when anyone who can leaves town, making the city easier to get around. *Dia de los Muertos* (November 2) is a great time to travel anywhere in Mexico to experience one of its most moving traditions.

Documents A passport is required to enter Mexico by air, and probably will be required soon for those arriving by car. Before leaving home, make Xerox copies of your passport, credit cards, driver's license and any other important documents and leave them with a friend. Better yet, scan your documents into a computer and send them to yourself as an e-mail attachment. Keep them in a permanent file in your e-mail account for access anywhere in the world.

Learn some Spanish While you can easily travel throughout Mexico without knowing the language—Mexicans are very helpful and accommodating—you will enhance your visit greatly with some basic Spanish. Learn a few greetings, numbers, words for ordering food and you will be surprised at the way Mexicans open up to you. Even if you speak badly, they usually make you feel like an expert. If you are uncomfortable with Spanish, ask someone at your hotel to write out names and addresses of your destinations to show taxi drivers. The website www.studyspanish.com is very useful.

Money ATMs (called *cajeros automáticos*) are found all over the city for getting pesos. Using your bank card is more convenient than traveler's checks or cash, and the exchange rate is often better. The same is true of credit card purchases, although credit cards are not accepted at many smaller stores and restaurants. Be alert when you enter and leave ATM booths—there are accounts of robberies.

Prices is Mexico are generally marked in pesos, but the $ is used before the number, confusing many Americans who think it means dollars. $50 means 50 pesos.

Airport Arrival When you get to passport control you will be given a slip of paper—your tourist permit. Hold on to this— you will need it to leave the country. Follow the crowd to Passport Control, then to claim your luggage, then on to Customs (*Aduana* in Spanish)—it is all clearly marked. At customs you will be asked to push a button which illuminates a red or green light at random. If you hit red your baggage will be searched, but in my experience this has been perfunctory. Through the doors in front of you is the Arrivals Area full of eager families and porters. There are lots of money exchange places and ATMs directly in front offering good rates.

Ask a porter to help you, even if you don't have much luggage—he can help guide you through the chaos. (A 10 to 30 peso tip is normal—pay when you get to the taxi.) Pre-paid registered taxis are available to leave the airport—DO NOT go out on the street to hail a cab without a ticket. Buy your ticket at the counter outside the Arrivals Area. If the airport is very busy, go right as you exit the customs area and go to the last door (*Puerta* 10, *Sala* F)— there is taxi ticket booth here that is usually less crowded. You will see the words *taxis autorizados* clearly marked, or ask your porter. Fares are determined by zones—just tell them where you are going. There are two windows for buying taxi tickets—one for regular cabs, another for vans and bigger vehicles, so make sure you get the size vehicle you need. The cab driver will take the ticket and give you half as your receipt. Sometimes there is an additional charge if you have lots of luggage, but a tip is not customary.

I use a taxi *sitio* that my neighbor Dolores, who works for the airlines, told me about. Walking toward Sala A you will see an overhead pedestrian bridge between *Puertas* 5 and 6. Take the escalator up and follow the sign for 'crew parking'. The sitio is at the far end of the bridge, down the stairs. Metered taxis here cost about half of those mentioned above. You can arrange to pay by the hour (around US$10)—having a taxi driver meet you at your hotel is a great way to see the city without further transportation worries. There is a metro stop at the airport, too. The entrance is outside, past Sala A. Large suitcases or parcels are not permitted on the metro. Caution: if you are taking the metro to the airport, the station is called Terminal Aerea on the Yellow Line (#5)–do not get out at the stop marked Aeropuerto. I have yet to figure out the logic of this.

Arrival by Bus Use the same system for getting a taxi as at the airport. Buy a ticket for your destination at the taxi kiosk. Use only these registered taxis—do not go out on the street and hail a passing cab. For bus travel, see the website www.ticketbus.com.mx, which offers tickets online to many destinations.

City Transportation I do not recommend renting a car for touring Mexico City unless you are familiar with the city or are a masochistic daredevil.

Taxis Taxis are everywhere in the city and fares are very reasonable. Stories abound of taxi-related crime, although in 10 years I have had no problems. My advice to first time visitors who do not speak Spanish is to use only *sitio* taxis (literally means "site" as they are found in specific locations marked by that word) which are registered and safe, or hotel taxis, which are more expensive but also reliable. Sitio locations are found in many of the more popular tourist destinations, or you can call them to pick you up anywhere in the city. If you find a cab driver you like, get his card so you can call him. Many drivers will work on an hourly basis (Around US$10to $15 an hour) which is a great way to see a lot of city quickly and easily. Sitio cabs usually charge by zone, although some use meters in the daytime. Drivers sometimes ask for a flat fee at night. It is very important to agree on a price beforehand if there is no meter. If a price seems exorbitant, it probably is: taxis are usually very reasonable in this city. Most destinations within the center city should be under 100 pesos. It's a good idea to carry a city map with you.

It is not customary to tip taxi drivers (unless they provide an extra service such as waiting or carrying your bags) but it is always appreciated.

Expect to pay more for *Taxis de Turismo*, which are found at hotels and some tourist sites, like the *Museo de Antropología*.

Here are a few *sitio* phone numbers:

- Servi-Taxi 5271-2560

- Radio-Taxi 5566-0077 or 5516-6020 or 5519-7690

- Sitio Parque Mexico 5286-7129

- Base Concord (at the airport) 5762-0756

If you do hail a cab on the street, take a few precautions. It is best to know where you are going and the mostly likely route by checking a map before you go. Every cab is required to have a visible license with a photo and a fare meter--don't enter cabs without these or with broken meters. I also look for a statue of the Virgin of Guadalupe on the dashboard for reassurance.

Do not take any cab that solicits you—advice that holds true worldwide. Always use sitio taxis if you are travelling with luggage.

If you are leaving a restaurant or club at night, ask someone to call you a taxi. Many nightspots have taxis out front known to the management—make sure the doorman or other person in charge indicates the cab for you. Carry a phone card with you to call taxis, or if you are here for a longer stay, you might consider buying a local cell phone, which can be purchased for as little as 350 pesos.

Buses, Peseros, Metrobus

There are thousands of bus lines in a Byzantine system. Small shelters on some corners indicate designated bus stops, but you can often get the smaller ones to stop just by waving your hand. Prices vary from 2 to 4 pesos–if you don't see a fare sign, tell the driver your destination and he will tell you the amount. Bus routes are indicated by their final destinations, posted in the front window. I find two basic lines most helpful in getting around the city.

Reforma is the major east-west thoroughfare—use buses here to get from the Centro Histórico to Parque Chapultepec and back. Look in the front window for Auditorio when going toward the park, and Hidalgo or Zócalo when heading toward the Centro. Insurgentes, the city's longest street, runs north-to-south the entire length of the city and beyond. The **Metrobus** along Insurgentes has stops at most major intersections. These are larger buses with a designated lane, so it's often the fastest way south (Coyoacán and San Angel for example). A ride down

THE METRO

About 4 million people take the metro every day making it a great place for people watching. Merchants and musicians pass through the cars, singing or selling their wares, altering their voices to high-pitched nasal sounds which sustain the vocal chords during long hours of work. A few vendors are children, at times disturbingly young, often unaccompanied by an adult. I once saw a young boy play the accordion while his sister passed the cup. Both of them were under 7 years old, but deep in their eyes they looked ancient. The *norteña* music he played was joyous and bouncy, creating an ironically upbeat soundtrack to a sadly poignant scene. *Gente* "Nice" (a mixed-idiom slang term for the well-dressed and well-bred) are rarely seen. A few of our Mexican friends, middle class and college-educated, have never been on the metro. I take the metro several times each week, often finding myself the tallest and whitest person in the car, but I have never felt uncomfortable.

Nothing bad has happened to me on the metro, but I stay alert, especially if it is crowded. Pay attention to your bags and pockets. Don't wear flashy jewelry. Keep cameras inside your bag, and keep bags and knapsacks in front of you. I never carry a wallet, just a photo ID, an ATM card, and enough cash for immediate needs–always in my front pocket. A Mexican woman friend rides the subway daily to work and never has problems. A tall blonde American friend who rode the subway alone became the object of unwanted sexual attention.

I will leave it up to women traveling alone to judge for themselves.

Insurgentes presents a good view of the burgeoning Mexican middle class, with lots of glitzy shopping and eating places, and some interesting new high-rise office buildings. Metrobus fare is 3.50 pesos. You must buy a rechargeable fare card before you board, sold from a machine at the entrance, which is good only on the metrobus. Be careful of the badly designed doors as they open and close.

Metro The metro is fast, efficient, clean, and cheap (2 pesos, less than 20 cents US). Nine different lines are both number and color coded. Trains are marked by their final destinations. Buy your ticket at the *taquilla* (ticket booth) and place it in the turnstile to enter. If you need to switch trains, follow the signs that say *correspondencia*. You will usually find metro maps on the wall near the *taquilla*, and maps by exit stairs show aboveground street plans. Cars at either end of the metro tend to be less crowded.

Avoid the metro during rush hours (7 to 10 AM and 6 to 8 PM) unless you love massive crowds I'm pretty sure it's the only metro in the world with real Aztec ruins. (The ruins of the Temple of Ehécatl, the

Aztec god of winds, can be seen at the Pino Suarez station.)

Bici-taxis Bicycle-taxi service is fairly new in the city and it is a delightful way to cover short distances in the Centro. Bici-taxis used to congregate around the Zócalo, but the city has been pushing them around, so they are a bit harder to find; you will notice them at major intersections in the Centro. Prices are determined by distance and weight: most rides within the Centro should be under US $5. You can also hire them by the hour (around 300 pesos/hour). Be sure to agree on the price before you start your ride.

Turibus A good way to see a lot of the city without worrying about transportation is to take the turibus (www.turibus.com.mx), a red double-decker that passes by most of the major tourist destinations. For about US $10 you can get on and off all day at 24 stops around the city. Headphones are available to hear commentary in several languages.

Asking Directions Mexicans do not like to say no, so they may give you directions even if they have no idea where you are going. I usually ask three people before I accept directions, unless someone seems extremely certain.

Planta Baja The first floor of a building is called the planta baja, the next floor is 1, then 2, etc.—in elevators you will see PB, which is usually the lobby or entry level.

Business Hours Most businesses, including markets, do not get rolling until 10 AM, so there's no need to hurry in the morning. Some smaller businesses close for comida (usually 2 to 4 PM), but this is increasingly rare. Most museums and all of Parque Chapultepec are closed on Mondays.

Magazines *Tiempo Libre.* This weekly magazine lists movies, theater, music, dance, art exhibits and more. It comes out every Thursday and is sold at most newsstands.

Chilango magazine has listings of what's going on in the city as well, and if you read Spanish, there are some fun articles on city culture. (The word "Chilango" is a formerly derogatory but now proudly worn slang moniker for a Mexico City dweller.)

Centro magazine is a walker's guide to the inner city, full of interesting detail and a good listing of current events.

Maps Be sure to get a good map of the city. *Guia Roji* makes the best maps as well as a detailed book of all city streets, indespensible if you live here. It is available at newsstands (at the airport and elsewhere), at Sanborn's, and at www.guiaroji.com.mx.

Government-run tourist kiosks located in the Zócalo, next to Bellas Artes, and in Parque Chapultepec are a good source for free city maps.

Telephones Telephone numbers within Mexico City have 8 digits. When dialing a Mexico City number from the U.S. or Canada dial 011-5255 before the 8-digit number.

If calling a Mexico City number from another part of Mexico dial 0155 before the 8 numbers. To call other countries from Mexico, dial "00" plus the country code ("1" for US). Most pay phones work with a card, which can be purchased at newsstands, pharmacies and stores displaying a LADATEL sign. It's a good idea to have one for calling taxis or possible emergencies; telephones that accept coins are hard to find these days.

A few important numbers:
Dial 060 for Emergencies
Dial 040 for Directory Assistance
Dial 5658-1111 for Locatel, a service which helps you locate anything, even if you don't have an exact name or address—very helpful.

Websites Some useful ones to find out what's happening:

- www.conaculta.gob.mx
- www. ticketmaster.com.mx
- www.ciudadmexico.com.mx
- www.mexconnect.com
- www.turiguide.com
- www.difusion.cultural.unam.mx
- www.fchmexico.com
  (Festival de Centro Historico in early spring)

Dress Mexicans are fairly casual in their dress, but always neat and clean, and relatively modest. At concerts or fancy restaurants you will see everything from tuxedos to t-shirts. Few Mexicans of either sex wear shorts in the city.

Smoking The concept of "no smoking" sections in Mexico is new and is found only in a few upscale restaurants, so don't freak out when the person next to you lights up—it is permitted

in most places. Non-smokers are sometimes seated at less desirable tables.

¡Aguas! (Literally "waters") means "watch out!" in Mexico. This warning dates from colonial times when, lacking a sewer system, dirty water would be thrown out of windows. If you hear it, look around you.

Heads and Feet Many Mexicans are short and the city is built to accommodate them. Watch your head! Especially in market areas, where sharp metal awnings appear unexpectedly. Watch your feet! Holes, cracks and bumps in the pavement are frequent.

Pedestrian alert I have found some of the worst and rudest drivers in Mexico. Generally kind and considerate, Mexicans can turn into *conquistadores* behind the wheel of a car. Do not take for granted any right-of-way. Cross streets carefully—pedestrians are considered nuisances to be ignored or challenged. There is no driving test to obtain a license in Mexico–take it from there.

Altitude Mexico City is about 7000 feet above sea level. Combined with polluted air, the altitude can affect some travelers. You might notice shortness of breath or tiring easily at first, but this usually passes in a day or two. Be careful with alcohol–at this altitude it packs more of a wallop.

Health Concerns Stories of "Montezuma's revenge" and other intestinal problems are not uncommon, but if you follow a few basic guidelines (see "Street Food" section below) you should be OK. NEVER drink tap water in Mexico. If you have diarrhea for more than two days, or if it is accompanied by fever, call a doctor. Dehydration can be a serious problem associated with diarrhea—drink some Pedialyte, available at most pharmacies, to restore electrolytes.
Do not eat fruits or vegetables unless they have been peeled or disinfected. However, you can assume that any restaurant mentioned in this book will be serving safe, clean produce and salads.

Safety If you follow common-sense rules of city behavior, you should be fine. Every visitor I have known has been positively impressed with how safe and inviting the city feels. Don't wear flashy jewelry or carry

expensive camera equipment openly. Be sure to read and understand the above section on taxis.

Bathrooms Things are much better than they used to be, but bathroom hygiene in Mexico is often not up to expected standards. Some bathrooms in public places have attendants. Americans can be baffled by this custom as such jobs don't exist in the first world. It is never an obligation to tip, but always appreciated. In markets, gas stations and some public places there is a charge of a few pesos to use the facilities. Be aware that toilet paper is often handed out near the entrance and may not be found inside the stalls.

Finding a bathroom while you are out and about: The Sanborn's chain can always be counted on for clean bathrooms. Hotels and department stores are also a good bet. I have made note of some of these in the Walking Tours.

Tipping and Bargaining Leave waiters 10 to 15% in restaurants. Taxi drivers do not expect tips, but it is always appreciated. Gas station attendants are tipped—a few pesos will do.

Many foreigners think that you must bargain for everything in Mexico, or pay in US dollars to get a better price. These are largely outdated concepts unless you are buying in quantity, or contracting a service such as a car and driver. Bargaining in most places will just make you look silly and cheap. Many travelers ask if they have paid too much for something. My advice is if you are comfortable paying the price, then the price is right.

Panhandlers The awareness of poverty in Mexico is never far from one's eyes, and while it is rarely oppressive, we are asked to help the needy often. Everyone must figure out his own strategy—mine is to give to the elderly and anyone who makes music.

Tranquility breaks The city can easily overwhelm the traveler with its intensity, so plan some restful breaks into your day. Churches are always good for relative quiet anywhere in the city. Take a walking tour of Colonia Roma or Condesa (especially tranquil on Sundays and holidays), or Coyoacán (better on weekdays), or walk through Parque Chapultepec (peaceful only during the week), or stop in a café.

A *limpia* in the Zócalo

WHERE TO SLEEP

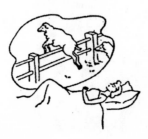

The Centro Histórico is the best location for first-time visitors. It is the heart of Mexico City where you can really feel its 700-year history. There is bustling street energy, Aztec temples, majestic colonial buildings, and great museums—all within a walkable area. If the frenzy of the Centro is too much for you, try one of the quieter neighborhoods listed below. Polanco and the Zona Rosa have many good hotels, but I find both areas lack distinctive ambience—you will feel more like you are still at home. You might find better rates at the more expensive hotels by booking on line, directly with the hotel or through websites such as www.hotels.com, www.expedia.com, or www.tripadvisor.com.

HOTELS IN EL CENTRO

For the traveler on a budget there are several options near the Zócalo, with rooms for under US$20. These places are usually pretty basic, but perfectly clean, with private bathrooms. Rooms tend to vary in these places—some have no exterior windows—so ask to see one first. Here are few to choose from:

Hotel Juárez (Cerrada de Cinco de Mayo 17, tel. 5512-6929)
Hotel Rioja (Cinco de Mayo 45, tel. 5521-8333)
Hotel Washington (Cinco de Mayo 54, tel. 5512-3502)

Hotel Gillow (Isabel la Catolica 17 at the corner of Cinco de Mayo, tel. 5518-1440). We used to stay here before we got our apartment. At under US$60 for a double, this place is a good deal. The best rooms on the 6th floor have terraces—there is an especially nice single room (#601) with a small terrace adjoining a church bell tower. They don't take reservations for the terrace rooms, however, so ask when you check in. (www.hotelgillow.com)

Hotel Catedral (Donceles 95, tel. 5518-5232). Owned by the same company, and in the same price range as the Hotel Gillow, this is the choice of several friends from San Miguel when they visit the city. There is a funny little terrace on the 6th floor with a view of the Cathedral where you can order food or drinks to be sent up. (www.hotelcatedral.com)

Gran Hotel de la Ciudad de Mexico (on the Zócalo, entrance on 16 de Septiembre, tel. 1083-7700,) This art nouveau masterpiece from 1899, with an impressive stained glass ceiling over the lobby, has been remodeled in standard fancy hotel style. The rooftop terrace has a great view of the Zócalo. Rooms start around US$275. (www.granhotelciudaddemexico. com.mx)

Hotel Majestic (on the Zócalo at Madero, tel. 5521-8600) has a lovely colonial style lobby and rooms starting at about US$130, but the ones facing the plaza will be noisy and lack good ventilation in hot weather. The rooftop terrace is a great place for breakfast or a drink. (www.hotelmajestic.com.mx)

Holiday Inn (on the Zócalo, entrance on Cinco de Mayo, tel. 5521-2121) has everything you expect (or fear) from Holiday Inns. Rooms start around US$90. The rooftop terrace has ugly

decor, but the view is great. (www.ichotelsgroup.com)

Tulip Inn (Madero 30, 2 blocks from the Zócalo, tel. 5130-0160) is a decently remodeled hotel with rooms starting around US$75. A good option if you don't want to be right on the Zócalo. (www.tulipinnritzmexico.com)

NH Centro Historico (Palma 42, tel. 5130-1850). This sleek new hotel is a few blocks from the Zócalo. There is a good view of the mosaics of the Correo Frances (p.36) from the restaurant. Rooms start around US$150. (www.nh-hotels.com)

Sheraton Centro Histórico (Avenida Juarez, facing the Alameda, tel. 5130-5300) is a modern high-rise affair, kind of glamorous, if a bit cold. It does have that big hotel buzz about it, and all the amenities you expect. Rooms start at around US$100 for off-season (on-line price) and go up to US$2000 for the biggest suite. (www.sheraton.com/ centrohistorico)

Hotel Bamer (Avenida Juarez, facing the Alameda) This 50's gem with great Alameda views is being renovated as I write … check for a new website on Google.

OTHER LOCATIONS AROUND TOWN

Hotel Maria Cristina (Rio Lerma 31, Colonia Juarez, tel. 5566-9688). This hotel is in a quieter residential neighborhood north of the Zona Rosa. The lobby has some charm and the rooms are clean and efficient. Prices start at around US$75. (www.hotelmariacristina.com.mx)

Camino Real Mexico (Mariano Escobedo 700, Colonia Anzures, tel. 5263-8888). Located near the entrance of Parque Chapultepec, this impressive hotel was designed by Ricardo Legorreta, one of Mexico's leading architects, who was inspired by the vast spaces of Teotihuacán. It has a fun big-hotel feel with flashy restaurants and bars, and a pool in a garden setting. Rooms start as low as US$105 off-season. (www.caminoreal.com/mexico)

W Hotel (Campos Elíseos 252, Polanco, tel. 9138-1800) If you want to stay in the most "fabulous" place in town, this is it. Here you will find high-end design and glamorous people. Prices start around US$250 (www.starwoodhotels.com)

Condesa DF (Avenida Veracruz 102, Condesa, tel. 5241-2600). This small, trendy hotel, with its hip decor, is where Paris Hilton and Damien Hirst have stayed. The restaurant and rooftop bar are hot spots on weekends, so ask about noise. Prices range from US$165 to US$395. (www.condesadf.com)

Hippodrome Hotel (Avenida México 188, Condesa) This place was set to open as this book went to print. This boutique hotel in the heart of Colonia Condesa is located in a lovingly renovated Art Deco apartment building—it looks like it will be something special. (www.stashhotels.com)

Hotel Roosevelt (Insurgentes Sur 287, corner of Yucatan, tel. 5208-6813) is the only real budget option in Colonia Condesa. It has ugly art on the walls, but it's clean and comfortable and conveniently located for exploring Condesa and Roma—many of our friends stay here. Rates start at under US$50 for two. Inside rooms are quieter. (www.hotelroosevelt.com.mx)

Hotel Milan (Alvaro Obregòn 94, Colonia Roma, 5584-0222) This is the best location in Roma, directly across from Casa Lamm. The renovated rooms are compact but pleasant, and a

good deal at around US$40 for a double.
(www.hotelmilan.com.mx)

Quality Inn Roma (Alvaro Obregón 38, Colonia Roma, 1085-9500, Opened in May 2006, this slick, modern hotel is comfortable and attractive—the best upscale choice in Roma, with rooms starting round US$70
(www.choicehotelsmexico.com)

La Casona (Durango 280, tel. 5286-3001). Located in Colonia Roma, but within walking distance of Condesa, this remodeled mansion offers comfort and old-style charm. Prices vary, but start around US$120. Check on-line for special offers.
(www.mexicoboutiquehotels.com/lacasona)

Hotel Century (Liverpool 152, Zona Rosa tel. 5726-9911). Advertising itself as the "gay friendly option", this hotel is near the gay nightlife scene of the Zona Rosa. It has a slightly faded elegance, but very clean rooms with a/c and a small pool on the roof with great views. Rooms cost about US$100, but check on-line for special rates.
(www.century.com.mx)

There are a few **private apartments** to rent for both long and short stays. through the websites www.VRBO.com, and www.mexicocity.craigslist.org.

If you are planning a long stay, check out the **Hostal Virreyes** (Izazága 8, Centro, tel. 5521-4180) which has monthly rates starting at under US$200, and attracts a hip, young crowd. Visit their amusing website:
www.hostalvirreyes.com.mx

For fully equipped and serviced apartments, visit www.homesuiteshome.com.
They have two good locations, one in Condesa and one off Reforma, near the Zona Rosa.

WHAT TO SEE AND DO

- Tour the Centro Histórico, the oldest part of Mexico City   p.19

- See the world's greatest collection of pre-conquest art at the Museo de Antropología   p.38

- Shop in a Traditional Mexican Market   p.42

- Explore the colonial era streets and markets of Coyoacán and San Angel   p.47

- Stroll through Chapultepec Park   p.55

- Tour a residential neighborhood: Condesa & Roma   p.58

- Glide down the ancient canals of Xochimilco and see the best collection of paintings by Frida Kahlo and Diego Rivera   p.71

LA RAZA

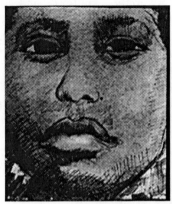

Watercolor by Esther Gilman, 1949

Past and present often inhabit the same space in Mexico City: the architecture, the food, the faces of the people reveal mixed races and conquered tribes. You hear the names: Tenochtitlan, Popocatepetl, Iztacihuatl, Nezahualcoyotl, Chapultepec, Moctezuma. Settled in 1325, it is the oldest city in the western hemisphere, a place founded on Aztec prophecy: an eagle, devouring a snake while perched on a cactus, was a messanger from the gods indicating the site of the city. This violent image, all thorns and claws, adorns the Mexican flag today.

Human sacrifice was among the rituals performed in their main temple, whose ruins you can see by the Zócalo. When Hernán Cortéz and his Spanish *conquistadores* took charge in 1521, they used stones from this very temple to build the imposing Cathedral next door. Mexican Catholicism, too, enveloped Aztec paganism, with statues and paintings graphically violent in ways rarely seen in European art. The basilica of La Vírgen de Guadalupe, the most revered religious site in all of Latin America, is built atop a shrine to the Aztec mother-goddess Tonantzín, and you will often find *conchero* dancers performing there in flamboyant Aztec costumes. In spite of the fact that Mexico is more than 90 per cent Catholic, one senses the conversion is not complete and that traces of ancient beliefs are lurking in the shadows.

CENTRO HISTÓRICO

The Centro Histórico is Mexico City's oldest area and the best starting point for any visit. It is the hub of government, religion, and commerce in Mexico, one of the liveliest and most beautiful parts of town. The area was heavily damaged by the earthquake in 1985, but recent investment is reviving the glamour that made it world-famous in the 1950's, when the young Maria Callas sang at the Opera and Diego Rivera and Frida Kahlo dined at the Hotel del Prado (destroyed in the 1985 quake). The two most important areas to explore are the Zócalo and the Alameda. As you are walking around be sure to look in every open door—the city is full of hidden surprises.

WALKING TOUR OF THE CENTRO HISTORICO #1: AROUND THE ZÒCALO

Officially known as Plaza de la Constitución (although nobody calls it that) this is the main square of Mexico City, one of the largest urban plazas in the world, and the political and religious center of the country since Aztec times. The Spanish name means pedestal: the story goes that a pedestal was put there by President Santa Ana in 1840, but the statue never arrived. The name stuck and is now used to define town squares all over Mexico.

Arriving by metro gives you a dramatic first view of the **Zócalo**—you will exit right in the middle of it (use the exit marked Plaza de la Constitution) On most days (if there is no concert or demonstration going on) the sound of drums will lead you to a group of *concheros*, men and women dressed in Aztec/Las Vegas outfits who dance, chant, and burn incense in the center of the plaza. Groups of concheros are seen in many Mexican fiestas and parades, mixing the past and present. Dance steps represent astrological formations. Concheros often fast beforehand to intensify the near-trance state sought through the rhythms and motions of the dance. You may also see people lining up for a *limpia*, ritual cleansing using incense and herbs to get rid of bad spirits. You, too, can do this—just put a few pesos in the cup afterwards. Enter the **Palacio Nacional**, which covers the entire east side of the plaza and houses the office of the President (you will need a photo ID to enter.) Montezuma's palace was in this very spot. Surrounding the stairwell are murals by Mexico's most famous artist, Diego Rivera, entitled "Epic of the Mexican People", painted between 1929 and 1935. Upstairs are more Rivera murals (painted between 1941 and 1952) depicting Aztec life before the conquest. The last mural depicts the Spanish conquistadores, shown in an unflattering way that leaves no doubt about Rivera's opinions. Guides are available to explain it all to you, but check that the one you hire speaks your language well—a few I have overheard were barely intellegible. There are public bathrooms on the ground floor.

Turn right as you exit the Palacio Nacional and walk straight (crossing Calle Moneda) to the ruins of the **Templo Mayor**, the main site of Aztec worship. The 45 peso entry fee (free on Sundays) gets you into the ruins and the museum next door. Being in the midst of the temple ruins, in the heart of the modern city, is a rich and evocative experience, a compression of 700 years of history—all the more amazing when you realize the ruins were only discovered in 1978 while electrical workers were laying new cables. At the Altar of Tzompantli there is a striking view of a small shrine covered with 240 stone skulls with the Cathedral as its backdrop. The small museum displays art works from this site; the life-size ceramic figures on the top floor are noteworthy. A huge stone disc representing the dismembered body of Coyolxauhqui (best viewed looking down from the top floor) is one of the most compelling works of Aztec art. Having killed her pregnant mother Coatlicue, she herself was killed by her own brother, Huitzilopotzli, who was born fully grown and armed for battle. This Coyolxauhqui is dressed to kill: check out her carved headdress, shoes, and skull belt buckle.

Walk back to the Zócalo where you will see the massive **Catedral Metropolitana**, the most important Catholic church in Mexico, begun in 1573, built using stones from the Templo Mayor. The smaller building on the right is the Sacristy, built almost 200 years later, whose neo-classical interior has recently been refurbished. It is slightly dull compared to its neighbor. The main Cathedral entrance brings you into the baroque splendor of the seat of Mexican Catholicism —lots and lots of gold. It is worth sitting down to view the main altar at the back of the church to absorb its imposing complexity. In the middle of the church is a lead weight hung from the ceiling which indicates just how far off-center the massive building is now, having sunk into the soft earth over the centuries

As you exit the Catedral walk right along the tall iron railing. At the corner you will see workers of many kinds, mostly electricians, plumbers, and brick masons lined up seeking employment for the day. Nearby is an information kiosk where you can pick up some decent maps. Next to that are a taxi sitio and the bus stop for the Turibus.

Cross the street to Avenida Cinco de Mayo. Be sure to look up as you walk along to notice some of the best architectural details. At Palma 13 (first street on your right) the small balconies are a lovely detail of Porfirian architecture, reflecting the French influence promoted by President Porfirio Díaz, dictator of Mexico between 1876 and 1911.

Just 2 blocks from the Zócalo (at the corner of Cinco de Mayo and the 2a Cerrada de 5 de Mayo) is **Jugos Canada**, with a wide assortment of refreshing fruit and vegetable drinks. It's one of my regular stops in the Centro. My favorites are *apio* (celery), *vampiro* (beet, carrot and orange juice), or a *licuado* (made with milk) of *guayaba* and *platano* (guava and banana.)

The Casa de Ajaracas (#46) and the Edificio Puebla (#43) both have interesting bas-relief decorations, which are called ajaracas. To the left at the corner of Isabel la Católica, you will see another slowly sinking church, San Felipe Neri. The **Cafe la Blanca** (Madero #40) has been around since the 1930's and has photos on the wall to prove it. They also have good café con leche. The 19th century **Dulceria de Celaya** (#39), with its beautiful painted glass sign, sells traditional Mexican sweets, such as crystallized fruits and candies made from sweetened goat's milk. The limes stuffed with coconut are my favorite—they are not as cloyingly sweet as they look. Notice the Aztec-Deco metal work at the Edificio Banco Mexicano (#35.) Other elegant buildings of the Porfirian era can be seen at #32 (Edificio Paris) and #20 (Edificio Cinco de Mayo).

At Cinco de Mayo #10 is the famous **Bar la Opera**. It's not much to see from the outside, so be sure to enter and see the beautiful wooden interior. The food is nothing special, but it is a great place to stop for a drink and hear music played by musicians who seem as old as the bar itself. Ask to see the bullet hole in the ceiling left by Pancho Villa during the Revolution.

Further down the block on the left is one of Mexico City's most famous and beautiful buildings, the **Casa de los Azulejos** (The House of Tiles.) This 18th century aristocratic residence, whose facade is completely covered with tiles, is now **Sanborn's**, a restaurant and store, the first location of a chain of stores now found all over Mexico. It is worth spending a little time exploring this magical place. The central patio is now a lovely dining area—a great place for breakfast or a light lunch (stick to the soups and simplest dishes—the enchiladas especiales are especially bad.) Be sure to go upstairs to see more of the tile work, and notice the ceiling over the staircase. There are clean public bathrooms up there too, and a mural by Orozco. Sanborn's also sells a good selection of books, maps, magazines and chocolates.

At the end of Cinco de Mayo you will see a building that looks like a big wedding cake. This is the **Palacio de Bellas Artes.** At this point you can start Walking Tour no. 2 to the Alameda Area. (p.25), or walk across Paseo de Condesa (alongside Sanborn's) to Calle Madero and follow this tour back to the Zócalo.

Across Madero from Sanborn's is a sculpture plaza with changing exhibitions. From this plaza is access to the **torre latinoamericana**, until recently the tallest building in the city. Take a ride up to the 44th floor mirador for the best aerial view of the city.

Next on Madero (following the direction of traffic) the church of San Francisco can be seen sinking into the earth. It has one of the finest baroque facades in the city; the interior is less interesting. Walk up to the front door and look back for a beautiful view of the rooftop finials on the Casa de los Azulejos.

At Madero #10 is **Victor**, a store with a fine selection of Mexican handicrafts, and lots of small gift items. You must walk through the perfume store and go upstairs to find it, but it's worth it. If you are a serious shopper, ask to see the other locked rooms with more expensive items for collectors.

Just past Victor is Calle Gante, a tree-lined pedestrian street with many outdoor restaurants and cafes. Go right on Gante and then right again on the next block (16 de Septiembre) to the **Pasteleria Ideal**, with its vast offerings of baked goods—worth a look even if you are not hungry. Be sure to go upstairs and see the display of outrageously decorated cakes for all occasions—this is one of my favorite surreal spots in the city (bring the camera), guaranteed to make you smile.

Walk back to Madero and continue to #17, the **Palacio de Iturbide**, one of the finest colonial buildings in the city, built around 1780. Cross the street to fully appreciate the ornately sculpted facade. Once the home of the first president of the Republic, later a hotel, it is now owned by Banamex and is often open to the public for art exhibits of high quality. Try to get upstairs to see the small chapel on the right with its lovely dome.

When you reach Calle Bolivar, turn right and go half a block to #27. Upstairs from the Borcegui shoe store is the **Museo del Zapato** (Shoe Museum), a surprisingly interesting place. Shoes from all over the world and from famous people are displayed. (Free entry, open M-F, 9-2 and 3:30-6)

At the corner of Madero and Isabel la Catolica you will see more fine examples of Porfirian architecture. Turn right and go down Isabel la Católica to #29 and visit the elaborate **Casino Español**, which now houses a restaurant and social club. Be sure to go upstairs and see the main salon facing the street.

Continuing along Madero, you will pass lots of jewelry stores. Upstairs at #60 is the Marisqueria Las Palmas, a seafood restaurant. It's a good place to try a *coctél de camarón* (shrimp cocktail, Mexican style).

Madero ends at the Zócalo. If you did not start with breakfast at the **Hotel Majestic** (entrance on Madero) be sure to see the lobby or take a break at their rooftop restaurant.

Turn right at the Zócalo and walk along the arcade, which dates back to 1524 and is the center of the jewelry business. Turn right at the next corner, 16 de Septiembre, and go into the **Gran Hotel de la Ciudad de Mexico** to see its spectacular lobby (just act important as you walk past the snooty lobby guards). It has been recently restored to show off the cast-iron work and Tiffany glass ceiling. There is a rooftop restaurant and bar here, too, both recently remodeled in business-like fashion.

This is the end of the basic walking tour of the Zócalo area.

If you want to continue the tour to the nearby **Alameda**, go back to the left side of the Cathedral to the taxi sitio or, even better, try and find a bici-taxi to take you to the Palacio de Bellas Artes.

Conchero Dancers at rest

WALKING TOUR OF CENTRO HISTORICO #2: THE ALAMEDA AREA

Start your tour at the **Palacio de Bellas Artes**, the giant wedding cake that is Mexico's main venue for opera, concerts and ballet. The building has sunk several feet below its original position. Begun in 1904 in French Belle Époque style, the Mexican Revolution put a stop to construction. When things started again in the 1930's styles had changed, thus creating the surprising mixture of Art Deco with Aztec influence (notice the heads atop the lobby columns, a reference to the ruins of Teotihuacán). A magnificent Tiffany glass stage curtain and a glass dome inside the theatre enrich the interior, which you can only see by attending a performance. There is a pleasant restaurant in the lobby. On the right side of the lobby, a bookstore and a small store selling cd's both have good selections by Mexican artists. Upstairs there are murals by Rivera, Tamayo and Siqueiros, among others, and a **Museum of Architecture** on the top floor-which is worth visiting for the views alone. You must buy a ticket in the lobby to go upstairs.

If you are interested in attending a performance at Bellas Artes—well worth it to see the inside of the theater—check the listings on the wall in the front lobby. Ticket booths are right there, too. The Ballet Folklórico offers colorful dance performances every Sunday and Wednesday. The website www.conaculta.gob.mx lists events at the Palacio de Bellas Artes, or check the magazines listed on page 7.

Directly across the street from the front door of Bellas Artes is a **Sears** store—the 8th floor cafe is a great place to enjoy the view of the gardens below—and the coffee is good, too. From this garden plaza there are interesting tourist sights in all directions; there is an information kiosk near Avenida Juarez at the corner of the park.

On the east side of the Palacio de Bellas Artes (the corner of Calle Tacuba and Eje Central) is the **Correo Nacional**, the main post office, completed in 1907. The recently restored interiors are a marvel of marble, cast iron and brass. An exhibit about the Mexican Navy is on the top floor, where there are some interesting rooftop views.

Diagonally across the street from Bellas Artes you will see the

Torre Latinoamericana, completed in 1956 and until recently Mexico's tallest building. It is one of the most important symbols of urban Mexico. In the lobby you can buy a ticket for the *mirador* (overlook) on the 44th floor, which, if the day is clear, provides astounding views of the city.

North of Bellas Artes (the back end) along Avenida Hidalgo is the Plaza de la Santa Veracruz, flanked by two churches and two good museums. This plaza is both charming and disturbing as you see, once again, how the buildings are sinking into the soft ground below. In one corner of the plaza is the excellent **Museo Franz Mayer,** housed in a restored 16th century building. There is a permanent collection of colonial and European art and interesting temporary exhibits as well. The café and garden is one of the most charming spots in the city. Try to get the table furthest from the food service area to appreciate the view of the church cupolas next door. If you do not wish to visit the museum proper, you can pay 5 pesos to enter the courtyard and cafeteria only.

Also on this plaza is the **Museo de la Estampa**, a small museum devoted to printmaking, which has a long and honored history in Mexico. On the street directly in front of this museum is my favorite tlacoyo stand (see p.80).

Just across the street is the **Alameda**, a pretty park with fountains that dates back to colonial times, when only the rich were allowed to enter. It is a great place to watch people, breathe some oxygen, and see the *policharros*, policemen on horseback wearing traditional Mexican garb. You might stop to get a shoeshine and watch the world go by. The Alameda is especially nice in late afternoon when the sunlight streams through the trees and makes the fountains sparkle.

At the far end of the Alameda (Juarez 89, near Balderas) you will find the **Fonart** store. This is the *Fondación Nacional de Artesanías*, a government-run store that features Mexican handicrafts from all regions of the country. If you are visiting in October, the annual exhibition of prize-winning crafts is displayed upstairs—well worth it for serious collectors of Mexican folk art.

To the left, across the street from Fonart, stands the high-rise **Sheraton Hotel** (good clean public bathrooms.) Down the street on the left side of the hotel (Calle Revillagigedo) is the **Museo de Arte Popular**, with a great collection of Mexican handicrafts, beautifully displayed, and a nicely stocked store. Opened in March 2006, it immediately placed itself as one of the finest museums in the city. The Art-Deco building has been lovingly updated; be sure to notice the Aztec-style bas-relief decorations outside. Their website is www.map.org.mx.

Across from the entrance to the Sheraton Hotel is a small plaza—sort of an annex to the Alameda, where you will find the **Museo Mural Diego Rivera,** which houses the famous "Dream of a Sunday Afternoon in the Alameda" from 1948. The mural was formerly in the lobby of the Hotel del Prado, which collapsed in the 1985 earthquake. Miraculously, the mural survived unscathed and was moved to its current home, an impressive feat of engineering which is chronicled inside.

Also at this end of the park is the **Laboratorio Arte Alameda** (entrance at Dr. Mora 7), a former church that has been turned into an enormous venue for video and installation art. Their website is www.artealameda.inba.gob.mx

Walking along Avenida Juarez (back toward Bellas Artes along the park) you pass a semicircular colonnade, the Monument to President Benito Juarez, Mexico's most honored ex-president. Directly across the street is **Patio Juarez,** an attractive new complex of government buildings, plazas and fountains designed by Ricardo Legorreta. The facade of a colonial church has been nicely incorporated into this modern plaza, which is used as an open-air art gallery

Continue along Juarez back to the starting point of this tour at the Palacio de Bellas Artes. The **Ghandi Bookstore**, one of the best in the city, is just across the street.

The nearest taxi sitio is at the Hotel Sheraton at the other end of the Alameda, or look around for a bici-taxi.

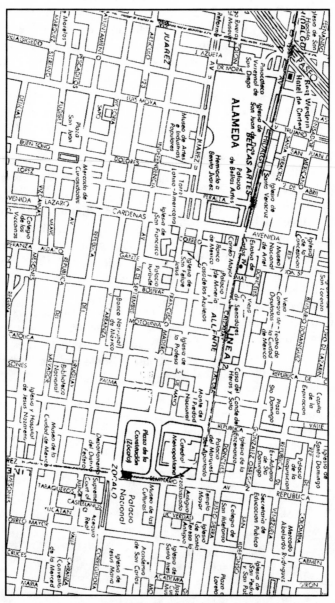

Map of the *Centro Histórico*

Organ grinder near the Alameda

WALKING TOUR OF CENTRO HISTORICO #3: BEHIND THE CATEDRAL

Starting at the Zócalo, walk along Calle República de Brasil, at the far left corner behind the Cathedral. Notice the small altar at no. 22 as you walk 3 blocks to **Plaza de Santo Domingo,** which is completely surrounded by imposing colonial buildings. Under the arcades are public scribes at typewriters and small printing businesses where hand-set type is still used. These same activities have gone on for centuries in this plaza. You can have business cards made here and pick them up a few hours later. At the far end of the plaza is the Church of Santo Domingo, which has several baroque altars covered in gold leaf. At the corner of República de Venezuela is the building which once housed the Spanish Inquisition. It is now the Museo de la Historia de Medicina (being renovated at the time of writing). Just inside the front door to the right is an exhibit of a real embalmed cadaver.

From the plaza, walk along Luis González Obregón, noticing the *ajaracas* (bas-relief decoration) at #14 and the beautiful tiled bell tower of the church just beyond that. When you reach the corner of Republica de Argentina, turn left and go half a block to #28, the **Secretaría de Educación Pública,** which has my favorite murals by Diego Rivera. There is a lot to see here, so I recommend that you start upstairs on the 3rd floor. The murals here were painted later than those on the ground floor and show a firmer compositional technique and mastery of color. They are perfectly fitted to the architecture: a long scroll with words from songs of the revolution unites the many small murals. There are clean bathrooms here on all floors. If you are visiting in March, you will see a fine display of jacaranda blossoms in the back patio. Turn right as you leave the building and walk a block and a half to the corner of Justo Serra— you will see the ruins of the Templo Mayor in front of you. Go left on Justo Serra. Half a block up on your left is the **Antiguo Colegio de San Ildefonso,** a former Jesuit college dating back to the 16th century. Today it is one of the city's finest museums, with changing exhibits, usually of high quality; but it is worth a visit for the architecture alone. (35 peso entry, free on Tuesdays, closed on Mondays)

After visiting the museum, exit left and continue along Justo Serra two more blocks to Plaza Loreto, turn right on Calle Loreto and go two more blocks to the corner of Callejón Amor de Dios (there is a small plaque with this name on the corner, but most maps will show it as Calle Moneda) where you turn right again. You will be passing by numerous street vendors (known as *ambulantes*) selling all kinds of cheap goods, much of it made in China. (If you are visiting in December or early January, you might want to skip this part of the tour and head back to the Zócalo if the crush becomes oppressive.) Vendors occupy dozens of streets in the area behind the Zócalo and represent an ongoing problem with the city government. There are regular raids by police which clean up the streets temporarily, but the ambulantes keep coming back. There is not much that you are likely to buy, but the atmosphere is lively.

As you turn right onto Calle Moneda you will see the ominously tilting Church of Santa Inés in front of you—not a particularly compelling place, but perfect for a tranquility break. On the opposite corner (entrance on Calle Academia) is the Academia de San Carlos, once Mexico City's most important art school, which has an impressive facade, but not much happening inside these days.

Continuing along Moneda you will see the Museo de las Culturas, which has a very pretty courtyard, but otherwise fairly didactic displays of pottery and other artifacts of world cultures. Just beyond that on your right is the small street **Licenciado Verdad**, whose name brings a smile to many Mexicans—a literal translation would be "Lawyer Truth". This street, a mix of decay and renovation, could have been dreamed up by Dickens. The site of the first printing press in the new world is on the corner, and next to that is Ex-Teresa Arte Actual, a deconsecrated church which shows trendy contemporary art. At the end of the street on the right is the Palacio de la Autonomía, a beautifully restored colonial building—be sure to get to the back of the building where you can walk on a glass floor over the convent ruins.

Back on Moneda (at no. 4) is the **Antiguo Palacio de Arzobispado** (Museo SHCP), until 1867 the home of the Archbishop of Mexico. The changing art shows here are usually worth a visit— the building, a massive thing which visually embodies the weight of Mexican Catholicism, certainly is. When the street vendors are in full swing, this spot is one of the sonic highlights of Mexico City. Close your eyes and imagine what an Aztec marketplace might sound like—I think this is it.

Just ahead of you now is the Zócalo. You might want to stop for a drink or snack, or just to look, at **El Nivel**, one of the oldest cantinas in the city (1855). It is a great place to watch people, including the waiters, and soak up the funky old-fashioned ambience. Located at Moneda 2, there is no sign and no number. Look for the brown doors—the last on the right before you reach the Zócalo where this tour ends.

Workers advertise their trades in the Zócalo

JUXTAPOSITIONS

Frida Kahlo`s paintings have shown the world a slice of Mexican surrealism, and the reality is not so different. One Friday afternoon I went to see an exhibit by Gabriel Orozco, a well-known contemporary artist, whose conceptual works are shown in museums around the world. Nick and I were the only two people there. Leaving the gallery (somewhat unimpressed by the cluster of battered soccer balls on display) we were walking along Paseo de la Reforma and saw a group of about twenty people looking up and pointing toward the sky. I asked what was going on. "It's a UFO" I was told, but looking up could see nothing but a beautiful blue sky streaked with cirrus clouds. With more help from a bystander I finally saw the miniscule white dot, but was baffled by how anyone could have seen it in the first place. A block away at the busy intersection of Insurgentes, Nick noticed that a man was removing his pants. Suddenly dozens of men were removing their pants and shirts. Soon hundreds were standing on the sidewalk in their underwear, pulling them down to expose their butts to passing traffic. Next to the statue of Cuauhtémoc (leader of the Aztecs after Moctezuma) nine rather fleshy women were removing all of their clothes and painting slogans on their bodies with white paint. It turned out to be a protest against the corruption of the governor of the state of Veracruz. No one seemed surprised but us.

Once in the Zona Rosa, a touristy area of restaurants, shops and offices, I saw that someone had made their home—a corrugated metal shack—on an abandoned lot between two highrise buildings, while the rest of the property had been turned into a corn field.

A late-night TV variety show I watched included segments about the Virgin of Guadalupe, erectile dysfunction, and a reading of poetry by Octavio Paz, all immediately followed by an advertisement for bullet-proof windows for your car.

La Muerte, woodcut, 1949 by Irving Berg

OTHER PLACES AND EVENTS OF INTEREST IN THE CENTRO

Museo Nacional de Arte
(Tacuba 8). Set on a narrow but majestic neo-classic plaza, this 1905 building houses the best collection of Mexican art in the city from the 17th to the 20th century, with temporary exhibits on the first floor. Noteworthy are the 19th-century landscape paintings of José Maria Velasco and the woodblock prints of José Guadalupe Posada. Check out the cast-iron staircase, too.

Joaquin Clausell's Studio Located on the 2nd floor of the Museo de la Cuidad de Mexico (#30 Pino Suarez near El Salvador.) This is a cool, calm oasis in the center of the city. Clausell (1896-1935), an impressionist/symbolist painter, had his studio in this building owned by his wife's family. For years he used the walls as his sketchbook and the result is a delightful rambling mural of doodles, sketches and small paintings. The room is air-conditioned and has comfortable armchairs. The main part of the museum downstairs has changing exhibits.

Plaza de Danzón (Plaza de la Ciudadela, metro Balderas on the #1 or #3 lines.) There is dancing in the street every Saturday afternoon (starting at noon). You will see hundreds of people of all ages engaged in *danzón*, a restrained and demanding form of ballroom dance with roots in Cuba and the Caribbean state of Veracruz. You can join in the fun with free group classes. I highly recommend this weekly event, which is oddly touching and heart-warming.

Centro de la Imagen (Plaza de la Cuidadela 2, metro Balderas on the #1 or #3 lines, www. conaculta.gob.mx/cimagen) This is the most important venue for photographic exhibits in the city. Part of the main library building, the space is an interesting mix of colonial and contemporary architecture.

Centro Cultural de España (Guatemala 18, just behind the Cathedral) has slick contemporary art exhibits and a sleek rooftop restaurant where you can sample Spanish-style tapas.

Teléfonos de México (Victoria 59), The main office of the phone company is one of the hidden Art Deco gems of the city—be sure to go inside.

El Corréo Francés (at the corner Palma and 16 de Septiembre), this turn of the century department store building is distinguished by impressive mosaic tile decorations above and below.

YWCA (Humboldt and Morelos). In need of some work, this is one of the best examples of Aztec-Deco architecture in the city.

Festival del Centro Histórico
Each year at springtime there is an international festival of cultural events at various venues througout the Centro, lasting several weeks. Check their website:
www. fchmexico.com.

Noche de Primavera
Since 2003 the city has celebrated the arrival of spring in the Centro Historico. From early evening to dawn on the Saturday nearest to March 21 dozens of performers take to the streets, plazas and even balconies of the Centro. It is a rare opportunity to see this part of town with no cars and some great entertainment.

MUSEO NACIONAL DE ANTROPOLOGIA

(Paseo de la Reforma in Parque Chapultepec, www.mna.inah. gob.mx) This is one of the great museums of the world, the most impressive collection of pre-Colombian art anywhere–don't miss it! The building, designed by Pedro Ramirez Vasquez in the early 1960's, is a fine piece of architecture, with many pre-Hispanic references expressed in a modern idiom. Proportions of spaces echo the peaceful vastness of Teotihuacán, decorative screens on the upper floor are updated versions of bas-reliefs from Mayan temples, a pond filled with papyrus and turtles in the patio recalls the lakes and marshes the Aztecs first encountered here. A stately fountain in the middle supports a dramatically cantilevered roof. All rooms open toward this central patio in classic Mexican style, but also have access to leafy garden areas behind each gallery. It is a pleasure to walk around this beautifully designed museum.

The collection is organized roughly in chronological order, starting on the right side. The first rooms trace early primitive culture (be sure to walk through the **Sala Preclásico** to the back garden and see a recreation of a *troje*, the typical wooden house of Michoacán.) The **Sala Teotihuacán** gives you a good idea of what awaits at the actual ruins, just outside the city limits.

There is too much here to take in during a single visit, so don't try. If your time is limited, I recommend you walk straight through the open patio to the far end and enter the **Sala Mexica**, whose sculptures and artifacts illuminate Aztec culture. It is the biggest and most important part of the museum's collection. The famous 'Aztec Calendar' (which is not a calendar after all) is here along with much surprising sculpture and jewelry, and interesting scale models of the city in Aztec times.

Culturas de Oaxaca

features the best polychrome pottery and some cartoon-like codices, long narrative scrolls of pre-hispanic origin.

Culturas de la Costa del Golfo

highlights include the mammoth Olmec heads, among the oldest and most impressive of pre-Hispanic artifacts. Figurative sculptures with laughing faces offer a surprising glimpse of humor.

Sala Maya The Mayan people, along with the Aztecs, produced the most refined and complex art and architecture in Mexico. Don't miss the carved stelae from Yáxchilan and the reproduction of a Mayan temple in the back garden.

Culturas del Occidente

has objects from Mexico's early western cultures, which predate the Aztecs by many centuries. Curious flattened figures from Nayarit and charming animal sculptures from Colima are standouts here, as are the many unusual pottery shapes.

Upstairs you will find exhibitions about the indigenous population of Mexico. Mexico has more than 56 different ethnic groups. Almost 2 million people still speak Nahuatl and one million speak Mayan. Typical houses, dress, items for daily and ritual use and handicrafts are displayed. What makes it more interesting is realizing that most of what you see here is still found in many parts of rural Mexico, and one can overhear Nahuatl being spoken even here in the city (lots of soft shhh sounds).

Museum admission is free on Sundays, so it gets crowded. The museum is open from 9am to 7pm (closed Mondays)—but the admission price goes up from 45 pesos to 150 pesos after 5pm when it is sure to be very quiet. There is a restaurant below the patio level.

If you are lucky you will catch the **Voladores de Papantla** performing across from the museum entrance in the park. Four men, whose feet are lashed to ropes on a 75-foot pole, slowly revolve downward as a fifth man dances and plays the flute on a small platform on the top, with no rope attached. What you see is an offering to the fertility god Xipe Totec, a ritual of the Totonac people from the state of Veracruz, who have been doing it for centuries.

A tourist information kiosk and a Taxi de Turismo stand are in front of the museum on Reforma and can also be hired by the hour (150 pesos), while a one-way trip to the Zócalo will cost you 120 pesos. The less expensive taxi sitio is a 5-minute walk along Reforma at Auditorio Nacional. There are frequent buses in both directions; buses marked Metro Hidalgo will take you to the western end of the Alameda, less frequent ones go all the way to the Zócalo.

A short walk from the Museo de Antropología is the **Museo Rufino Tamayo** (www.museotamayo.org), housed in another beautiful building, which was awarded the 1981 National Art Prize. The experience of walking through this building makes a visit worthwhile. Tamayo, one of Mexico's most important 20th-century artists, donated a large collection of works by many artists to the museum, but you don't often see much of his own work there. Temporary exhibits change every few months.

The nearby **Museo de Arte Moderno** is across Reforma from the Museo Rufino Tamayo. The highlight here is the collection of 20th century Mexican artists, including the famous "Las Dos Fridas" of Frida Kahlo.

AMIGOS

To say that Mexicans are warm and friendly may sound like a cliché, but it is hard to deny. People are polite, often kind, and always patient. Modes of etiquette and social behavior exist in Mexico that have disappeared, or never existed, in many societies. When entering a store, for example, exchanges of *buenos dias* or *buenas tardes* are common, and upon leaving one often hears *que le vaya bien*, literally, "may it go well to you." In restaurants you will hear strangers saying to one another *buen provecho* (like "*bon apetit*"). Men shake hands upon meeting, and hugging is common among friends. It is customary for men and women friends to kiss cheeks, sometimes even upon first introduction. Young lovers in parks and metros are openly affectionate; couples in restaurants will sit next to one another, not across from one another. References are made to physical qualities, as terms of endearment. Anyone with light hair or skin will be called *güera* (or *güero* for men). Chubby friends will be called *gordo* or *gorda*. An African-American friend of mine is called *negrita* ("little black girl") when she shops in the market. Spanish spoken in Mexico reflects this tenderness with the softening use of the diminutive-*ita* or-*ito* after many nouns, as when a waitress once offered me "*azucarcito para mi cafecito*" (little sugar for my little coffee). Once you get used to all this social lubrication, much of the rest of the world seems very rude indeed.

VISIT A TRADITIONAL MEXICAN MARKET

If you have already been to the Museo de Antropología, you may have seen the diorama recreating an Aztec market. You can visit the real thing today and see how little has changed in 500 years. I include this in my book not as a shopping experience, although you are unlikely to leave empty-handed, but as a cultural one. More than just a place to buy groceries, it is part of a traditional way of life that is gradually changing as more American-style supermarkets appear on the scene—so go while you can. Many individual vendors, usually all of a family, join together to create these markets, which accounts for an old-fashioned village ambience.

Mexicans have a particular knack for displaying fruits and vegetables, arranging avocados in gravity-defying piles, cutting pink grapefruits like origami, splaying a ripe pomegranate into glistening segments. Meat and fish vendors might make many foreign visitors queasy–no plastic wrap and styrofoam separate you from the reality of the dead animal. Although today's markets offer sneakers, t-shirts and mountains of cheap stuff made in China, you can still find traditional handicrafts such as pottery and baskets for sale. At holiday times, especially Easter, Day of the Dead and Christmas, markets are filled with traditional foods and decorations.

Some of the best prepared food is found inside and around markets. You can find tamal and tlacoyo stands outside of market buildings, and inside there is usually a group of *fondas* (small eateries) serving inexpensive traditional Mexican fare. Close your eyes and listen to the sounds in the market, too. *Pregones* are the traditional calls that vendors cry out urging one to buy. "*¿Qué va a llevar?*" (literally "what are you going to carry away?") or "*¿qué le damos, marchanta?*" ("what can we give you, customer?") are among the many phrases that will be repeated often as you pass by.

Every neighborhood in Mexico City has its market, but a few are standouts: The Mercado Jamaica and La Merced, my two favorites, are described below. Other important markets are in Coyoacan (p.49), Xochimilco (p.72), Colonia Roma (p.66), and the Mercado San Juan in the Centro (p.93).

Mercado Jamaica (Jamaica is pronounced "ha-MA-ee-ka") is located at the corner of Avenida Morelos and Congreso de la Union, about a mile south of the Zócalo. This is my favorite market in Mexico City, the most colorful and picturesque of them all. As well as a produce market, this is the city's wholesale flower market; I come here every few weeks to stock up on flowers. Any taxi driver will know it, but it's an easy place to reach by metro—the Jamaica stop is on the #9 train. Look up to see the big Mi Mercado sign (all Mexico City markets have this same sign) at the corner of the market building and start there. The main building is a big concrete and tin bulk painted turquoise and green. The attractions here are a good selection of basketry at one end, some elaborate fruit baskets, a beauty parlor run by transvestites, and a stand selling tepache, a traditional drink of slightly fermented pineapple juice. But the most interesting parts of the market lie beyond this in several open-sided buildings. There is a stall with rare tropical fruits, one with many kinds of eggs, another offers different kinds of mole in paste form, and several displays of household items made of day-glo plastic. Look up to see paper maché piñatas and all kinds of market bags for sale—they last forever and make good gifts. This market is rarely crowded, making it much easier to manoeuver than most.

As you wander further on you will discover the **main flower market** of Mexico City, the real highlight of this place—row after row of vendors selling mountains of seasonal flowers at extremely low prices, open 24 hours a day, 365 days a year. It always dazzles, even more so during holidays, with colors and scents in hedonistic excess. Around Valentine's Day and Mothers' Day, roses of every color fill the aisles up to your shoulders; truckloads of golden marigolds and purple-red cox-combs arrive for Day of the Dead. Armfuls of pure white calla lilies (famously painted by Diego Rivera) are on sale, as are black gladiolas and daisies dyed sky blue. There are flowers for every occasion between birth and death. Over-the-top arrange-ments might incorporate fruit, plastic dolls, and even live gold-fish, with vivid color combina-tions you would not find anywhere but Mexico. There are vendors selling inexpensive vases, too, so you can buy flow-ers for your hotel room, or to bring to a friend.

This market is famous for its huaraches—not the kind you wear, the kind you eat. Masa (the corn dough used to make tor-tillas) is formed into long ovals—more or less the shape of a shoe, hence the name. Cooked on a griddle and topped with meat, cheese, or eggs, you will see them being aggressively sold in the covered market building. **El Huarache Azteca** (Calle Torno 166) across the street from the market which has been serving huaraches since 1940, is a better choice than the market stalls, many of which look too greasy for me. You can sit and watch huge mounds of dough being kneaded and formed into huaraches as you eat.

There is a taxi sitio behind the flower market; just ask if you don't see it.

La Merced Truly the mother of all markets, this massive conglomeration of buildings covering several acres has been active since the 17th century, when the area was crisscrossed by canals and goods were delivered in canoes. The commercial frenzy extends for blocks and blocks toward the Zócalo with wholesale merchants selling just about anything you can think of. The area lies 1km southeast of the Zócalo. Just ask any taxi driver to take you to La Merced, or better yet, ride the metro. Take the #1 train to the La Merced stop. If you exit at the front end of the train, you will be right in the middle of the main market building. It's the best way to arrive. Exploring in any direction, you will find piles of banana leaves and corn husks for making tamales, walls of dried chillies, mountains of garlic, large cylinders of stacked nopal cactus paddles, wild mushrooms, exotic fruits and vegetables, herbs, spices, mole—just about anything edible produced in Mexico, in huge quantities. Near the metro exit is a wide staircase leading to a lower level—the sign says *"desnivel"*—where you will find dry goods including baskets, metalwork and traditional Mexican costumes for children. Outside this huge main building are several smaller buildings, each with a different specialty. The ones for sweets, fake flowers and kitchen ware are fun for the staggering quantity of goods on display.

La Merced can be one of the most hectic places in the city, but if you move in a relaxed way, it can be a lot of fun. If you already feel overwhelmed by Mexico City, however, this market is not for you. It is best visited between 9 and 12am—it can get uncomfortably crowded after that, especially on weekends.

Along the west side of the main building are many food stalls. Check out one that looks clean and try some quesadillas of *flor de calabaza* or *huitlacoche*.

For a moment of tranquility, visit the nearby **Templo de San Tomás** la Palma, between the candy market and the artificial flowers—ask any vendor for directions.

If you still have some steam left, you might want to visit the **Mercado Sonora**, a few blocks from La Merced, (crossing Fray Servando at the pedestrian overpass.) It is commonly known as the witches' market. In the first few aisles on the left vendors sell herbs, folk medicines, candles, voodoo dolls, amulets and all sorts of things for casting spells to get rich or fall in love. Interest in this culture seems to be lessening over the years, but there is still enough here to make it worth a look.A few aisles over you can find some good traditional pottery (mixed in with lots of hideous new things) and an unappealing section of caged animals.

TIANGUIS

The Nahuatl word tianguis defines the once-a-week neighborhood street markets that have been a fixture of Mexico City life since Aztec times. Rooted in pre-automobile society, the store comes to you, usually once a week in most residential areas. Vendors set up tarp-covered *puestos* in the street, supplying all

your basic household needs. Neighbors come to shop and eat in an atmosphere of festive bustling, suddenly turning the city into a village. There is an especially attractive and clean tianguis in Colonia Condesa on Tuesdays.

COYOACÁN

About 10km south of the Zócalo is the village of Coyoacán ("Place of the Coyotes" in Nahuatl), which, although long since swallowed up into the greater metropolis, still preserves an aura of small town colonial charm. Near to the University, it is a favored place for professors to live, adding to its reputation of bohemian sophistication. Frida Kahlo's big blue house is here, as well as one of the best traditional markets in the city. Visiting Coyoacán during the week is a peaceful event; weekends have a fun, bustling atmosphere.

Arriving by metro (#3 train to the Viveros stop—don't be tempted to get out at the more logical Coyoacán stop), use the exit marked *Viveros de Coyoacán.* You will be on Avenida Universidad, walking against the direction of the traffic. Walk two blocks (crossing Progreso) until you reach a small stone bridge (no street sign). Cross over the bridge, head a bit to your right and walk down Calle Parras, which is lined with high-walled homes and secret gardens. Turn right when you reach Salvador Novo, then left on **Francisco Sosa,** one of the principal streets in Coyoacàn. (If you arrive by taxi, start the tour here, Francisco Sosa and Salvador Novo). At this corner is Casa Alvarado, an 18th century residence decorated with *ajaracas*, bas-relief patterns that are a characteristic of local colonial architecture. A mini-plaza across the street offers a better view of the house, and you can peek into a keyhole here and see one of the vast hidden garden spaces of Coyoacán. As you walk along Francisco Sosa, you will pass a few art galleries, a cake store, and a charming tiled-cupola at no. 292. The small Apapacho Galería at no. 258 shows work of well-know Mexican graphic artists at reasonable prices. As you pass no. 238 notice the size of the trees which gives away the age of this ancient neighborhood.

A bit further ahead is **Plaza Santa Caterina,** one of the most charming spots in the city, best experienced from one of its park benches. Across the street, you can walk into the lovely garden of the Casa de la Cultura Jesús Reyes Heroles, a cultural center in a former private home. There are more ajaracas (those bas-relief decorations) at #218. There is a small church and a couple of charming places to eat on the plaza as well.

If you want to conserve on walking, you might hail a taxi here and ride to the central plaza of Coyoacán—about 6 blocks further along Francisco Sosa (same direction as traffic).

If you walk, you pass by more imposing colonial era buildings. You might stop at the Instituto Italiano de Cultura (#77) or Los Talleres (#29), a dance school—both of them have charming back garden cafes.

You will see yellow arches straight ahead of you as you reach the main plaza, which is divided in two halves, **El Jardín Centenario** and **Jardín Hidalgo**. On weekends, the first part is filled with vendors selling crafts and hippie paraphernalia. On the left side is an aquarium that kids will enjoy and Sanborn's (clean bathrooms). On the right side is a good Uruguayan/Italian restaurant, Entrevero.

Straight ahead you will see the main church of San Juan Bautista, a gilded baroque affair. This part of the plaza has vendors selling balloons, toys and traditional sweets and is pleasant to stroll around or just sit and watch the world go by. Across the plaza to your left is the so-called **Casa de Cortez**, which

occupies the site of Cortez' home, but the actual building dates from 1755. Today it houses municipal offices, including a tourist bureau.

At the far end of the plaza (behind the church) you will see **La Guadalupana,** a cantina in business since 1932, once a favorite hang-out of Frida Kahlo and Diego Rivera. Just behind the restaurant on the right (Calle Higuera) is the Mercado de Antojitos, where you find many traditional Mexican foods. There are several stands with good pozole, and at #14 the best deep-fried quesadillas I have eaten— try *flor de calabaza* (squash blossom flowers) or huitlacoche (corn fungus.)

Walk down Avenida Hidalgo to the left of La Guadalupana. Half a block down is the **Museo de Culturas Populares** (closed Mondays), which has excellent temporary exhibits on various aspects of Mexican culture as well as a good bookstore. For a week around Candelaria—February 2—they sponsor a festival of tamales, with different kinds from all over Latin America (check their website for dates www.culturaspopulare-seindigenas.gob.mx, or look in Tiempo Libre magazine).

Head back to the corner of the main plaza, turn right on Allende and walk 3 blocks to the main market. Along the way you will pass the restaurant El Morral, a good choice for traditional Mexican dishes (excellent hand-made tortillas.) and Café El Jarocho where they have been roasting coffee beans since 1953.

The **Coyoacán market** is one of the most picturesque in the city and it has some of the best market food, both indoors and out—it's a good place to try tlacoyos. Enter by Puerta 9 and walk straight ahead to the middle of the market to find the justly famous **Tostadas Coyoacán** (don't get confused by the nearby competitors who are not as good). Crisp tortillas are piled up with a variety of ingredients which you will see laid out on the counter—try to get a seat nearby so you can ask what each one is. A big selection of fresh-fruit aguas frescas is available, too. In one corner of the market you will find baskets, pottery and bird cages for sale. Another corner features a popular out-door seafood restaurant with long communal tables.

Leaving the market, continue along Allende two blocks to Londres, where you will see the

Museo Frida Kahlo with its famous blue walls. There is a better collection of her work in the Museo Dolores Olmedo in Xochimilco, but the house and garden are interesting, and for Frida fans it's a must-see. You can usually get a cab outside the museum, or walk back to the plaza.

Sitio de Taxis On the plaza, behind the cathedral, where Higuera begins you can get a safe taxi to any destination. (tel. 5554-6224). You might consider engaging a driver by the hour here (about US$10 per hour, 3 hour minimum) to visit nearby San Angel or (a bit further) Xochimilco.

OFF THE BEATEN TRACK IN COYOACÁN

The **Cineteca Nacional** at the northern edge of Coyoacán (Avenida Mexico-Coyoacan 389, near Rio Churubusco—take a taxi or walk from Metro Coyoacán) shows an interesting mix of inter-national films, new and old in a 8-theater complex with bookstore and café. Look for listings in Tiempo Libre magazine.

Plaza de la Conchita A few blocks from the main plaza (walk down Higuera) is the lovely, peaceful park and church of la Conchita. This crumbling gem is a rare example of *tequitqui*, which shows the influence of indigenous Indian craftsmen on Spanish baroque architectural ornament.

Museo León Trotsky (Rio Churubusco 410 near Gomez Farías) The famous Russian revolutionary leader lived in Mexico from 1937 until his assassination in 1940. His house was left untouched since then—you can still see the bullet holes.

Museo Diego Rivera Anahuacalli (Calle Museo #150, Colonia San Pablo Tepetlapa, tel. 5617-4310, www.diegorivera.com/visit) Rivera built this studio and museum space, a few miles south of Coyoacán, incorporating distinctive elements of pre-hispanic architecture. The building is fascinating, as is his fine collection of pre-Hispanic art. If you are visiting around Dia de los Muertos, you will see one of the city's most elaborate altars. From Coyoacán, the museum is best reached by car or taxi, but you can take a bus down Avenida División del Norte, getting off at Calle de Museo—it's a bit of a hike from there.

El Rincon de la Lechuza (Alvaro Obregón 34, near Insurgentes) is a popular taco restaurant, known for their tacos al pastor.

Coyoacán and San Angel both lie in the far south of the city and are easily visited on the same day. When I go from Coyoacán to San Angel, I often stop for coffee and shopping at Librería Ghandi along the way. (Miguel Angel de Quevedo near Avenida Universidad). Books in English are limited, but there is a good selection of art, travel and design books, magazines, and all kinds of CD's and DVD's.

La Malinche by Diego Rivera

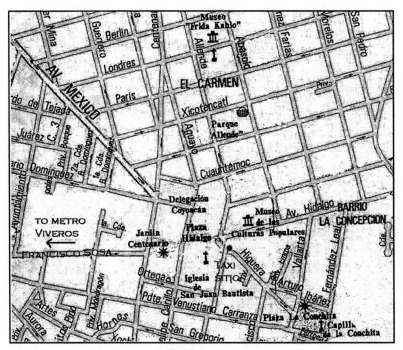

Map of Coyoacán

SAN ANGEL

Like its neighbor Coyoacán, San Angel retains its small town feeling with cobblestone streets and an attractive colonial-period plaza, although the commercial crush of the city impinges a bit more here. If arriving from Coyoacán, take a taxi or a bus heading west on Miguel Angel de Quevedo; if coming from the Centro, take a taxi or the metrobus down Insurgentes to Avenida de la Paz (Bombilla stop on metrobus), where this walking tour begins. Walk along Avenida de la Paz (you'll see Starbucks at the corner) toward the center of San Angel. There are several good restaurants on this street (see Paxia, p.92) and a very good book store, Las Sirenas, (inside the mini-mall at no. 57).

When you reach busy Avenida Revolución, go left to visit the **Museo del Carmen**, a 17th century convent and one of the treasures of colonial architecture in Mexico City. The sheer bulk and weight of the building creates wonder about the life the nuns must have led here. It has a good collection of religious art—and a cellar with some mummified nuns! After visiting the museum, bravely cross Avenida Revolución, which slashes the Plaza del Carmen in two, and walk along the left side of the park until you reach the **Plaza San Jacinto**, the main plaza of San Angel.

Passing a taxi sitio on the right side of the park, you come upon the Centro Cultural Isidro Fabela, also known as **la Casa del Risco**, which has temporary exhibits and a good collection of colonial art and furniture. Don't miss the fountain in the patio, a fantasy of ceramic plates and sea shells. Entry is free.

At the far left corner of the plaza (no.18 bis) enter the **Parróquia de San Jacinto** and wander through the red and white cloister, serene gardens, and the gilded baroque chapel.

Exit through the church garden, turning left on Juarez and left again on Arboles. A third left turn will bring you to the 2a Cerrada de Frontera, which leads to the intimate **Plaza de los Arcángeles,** a tranquil residential enclave, rather dreamy, especially when the jacarandas are in bloom. The Cerrada on the other side of the park will lead you to Frontera—go left here to return to the main plaza (Plaza San Jacinto). When you are ready, take a sitio taxi to the beautiful, old **San Angel Inn** a former hacienda (Diego Rivera 50). www.sanangelinn.com.

This is a good place for lunch or just to look around. Across the street is the **Museo Casa-Estudio Diego Rivera y Frida Kahlo**, Rivera's last home, designed by Juan O'Gorman in 1931. The architecture is interesting and looking at the personal artifacts of Rivera's life feels like good snooping. The doorman at the restaurant can call you a taxi when you are ready to leave.

OFF THE BEATEN TRACK IN SAN ANGEL

Bazar Sábado Often mentioned in guidebooks, this Saturday street market has lots of touristy handicrafts and even more ugly art, but the atmosphere is festive.

Museo Carrillo Gil (Av. Revolución 1608 at Altavista, www.macg.inba.gob.mx), has changing exhibits of contempory art, as well as a small but impressive collection of 20th century Mexican masters.

Museo Soumaya is about a half mile south of the center of San Angel in Plaza Loreto, an interesting shopping mall built in an old paper factory. There are changing exhibits of high quality, and the biggest collection of sculptures by Rodin outside of France. www.museosoumaya.com.mx

Taberna de León (see p.92), also located in Plaza Loreto, is one of the best restaurants in San Angel.

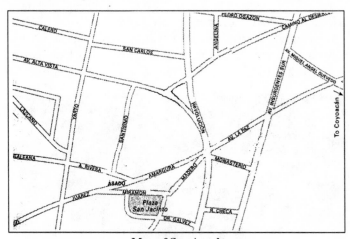

Map of San Angel

CROWDS

Mexicans enjoy being in groups, and move easily through crowds, rarely pushing, shoving, or yelling at each other. Public behavior is usually contained, but great value is placed on heartfelt emotion. Grief and joy are expressed with exuberance that would be considered crass in some societies—wailing cries are heard in mariachi songs and actors in *telenovelas* (Mexican soap operas) burst into tears every few minutes. Fiestas, both public and private, are a regular part of life. Even death is celebrated with much ado—*Dia de los Muertos* being one of the most important holidays of the year. Anger, however, is not considered appropriate for public display, and "saving face" is very important. Mexicans do not like to say no, which can cause much confusion with foreign visitors. For example, it is considered more polite to accept an invitation to a party and not show up than to refuse the invitation.

The relationship to time is another element that distinguishes Mexican life. The saying "Time is money" makes no sense here—they are two very distinct concepts. Being late for most social engagements is not considered rude, and speed is not highly valued (except in one's car.) One of the few instances where the foreign visitor will notice speed is at the end of a meal in a restaurant. Waiters often whisk away plates while the last bite of food is heading toward your mouth, so watch out; however, you are always invited to remain at the table for as long as you like, and a check is rarely presented without being requested).

PARQUE CHAPULTEPEC

The city's largest green area was a forest refuge even before the Aztecs arrived, and the first Spanish viceroy, Antonio de Mendoza, officially designated it a public park over 400 years ago. It is best visited on weekends to watch the people and the vendors—mingling with Mexican families enjoying a day off in the park is one of Mexico City's pleasures. There are several good museums here and a zoo that kids will enjoy. The Park is open from 5 am to 5 pm every day except Monday.

The main entrance to the park is on Reforma just opposite the Torre Mayor, Mexico's tallest building—use the underpass marked *paseo de peatones* from this side. If you arrive by metro (Chapultepec stop on #1 line), follow the exits marked Bosque de Chapultepec or Castillo and cross over the pedestrian bridge into the park.

Huge white columns flank the park's entry, a monument to *Los Niños Heroes*, the young cadets who defended the hill against invading Americans in 1847. There is a stately view of the Castillo from here. The **Museo de Arte Moderno** will be on your right (this back entrance is not always open., the main entrance is on Reforma) There is an important permanent collection of 20th century Mexican paintings and sculpture here, as well as temporary exhibits.

On your left is the entrance road to the **Castillo de Chapultepec**, which you can see at the top of the hill. These are the "Halls of Montezuma" referred to in the Battle Hymn of the Republic. The oldest parts of the building date back to 1785, but its historical importance to Mexicans is as the final holdout in the American War of 1847, when six young cadets (the famous "Niños Heroes") wrapped themselves in the Mexican flag and jumped to their deaths rather than surrender to the Americans. There are streets and even a metro stop named after Los Niños Heroes. In the 1860's the ill-fated Hapsburg Emperor Maximilian and his wife Carlotta remodeled the Castillo as their home, introducing elegant European furniture and gardens. Maximilian was also responsible for the Paseo de la Reforma, which he created as a grand promenade, modeled on the Champs Elysees, between his home and the government offices on the

Zócalo. President Porforio Díaz lived here, too, but since 1940 it has been a museum. The building has two sections. The **Alcázar** contains the residential quarters, carefully restored in period style, and formal gardens. In the dining room, notice the elaborate menu from a meal served in 1889; the bathrooms and the stained glass are also noteworthy. The other section is the **Museo Nacional de Historia**, with artwork and documents about Mexican history. Don't miss the impressive murals by Siqueiros, Orozco, and, my favorite, Juan O'Gorman, three important artists of the muralist movement of the 1920's through the 1940's. The best part of a visit to the Castillo is the 360-degree city view. A 10-peso train ride will get you up the hill if you don't feel like walking. The entry fee is 45 pesos.

Descending the hill, continue along the main walk. Follow the sound of the vendors until you reach the lake (where you can rent a boat if you like) then turn right toward the Museo de Antropología, where there is a taxi sitio. You will see signs for the Zoológico here, too.

As you exit the park facing the Museo de Antropología, check out the metal fences along Reforma. They are used for impressive outdoor photo exhibitions that change every few months.

If you are going to nearby Colonia Condesa after visiting the park, return to the metro. Use the pedestrian underpass and take the exit marked Calz. de Tacubaya—don't go through the turnstile. You will be near the end of Avenida Veracruz—from here you can follow the Condesa walking tour.

LA TIERRA

A walk anywhere in town will make one thing obvious—the earth is none too stable here. Lurching slabs of concrete, meandering cracks, and unexpected gaps in the pavement are everywhere, even along elegant Paseo de la Reforma. Roots of sturdy rubber trees burst through concrete and massive colonial churches tilt and sag into the soft ground. The city has a feel of a drawing done with an unsteady hand. Built on a lake in Aztec times, the land was bundled together into many small islands, like Venice. (You can still see this original landscape in Xochimilco.) Since the Aztecs did not use the wheel or pack animals, boats became a primary means of transport. Long since paved over, the soft liquid substructure of the city is still evident on its surface, rattled by occasional seismic activity. Scars from the deadly earthquake of 1985 are still found in parts of the city.

The physical instability has created a flexible and resilient culture. Mexicans are the most Buddhist-like of westerners, embracing instability, change, and death as normal parts of daily life, and as a result they seem remarkably calm. The phrase *"ni modo"* (literally "no way," sort of a resigned shrug) is more often heard in response to situations beyond one's control than anything more aggressive or confrontational. A popular song by the beloved ranchera composer José Alfredo Jimenez has the refrain *"no vale nada la vida"* (life is worth nothing), sung to a sweet and lilting waltz melody. Mexicans of all ages know it well.

TOUR A RESIDENTIAL NEIGHBORHOOD

The word *colonia* means neighborhood, and Mexico City has hundreds of them, as well as hundreds of *barrios*, which are divisions of colonias, usually defined by a particular saint's church. The feeling of small town life persists in many colonias, and you learn much about the city by visiting one. The following walking tours take you through Condesa and Roma, my two favorite neighborhoods.

WALKING TOUR OF COLONIA CONDESA

Colonia Condesa, a residential area inaugurated in 1925, is one of the loveliest parts of Mexico City, which is why we have chosen to live here. It is a neighborhood of parks and tree-lined streets, art deco houses, sleek modern apartment buildings, cafes and restaurants. It attracts artists, actors, writers, yuppies and foreigners. It is the perfect place to visit when the city starts to feel too much to handle and is especially tranquil on Sundays

and holidays. If you visit on a Tuesday or Friday you can see the weekly tianguis (see p.46).

Take a taxi to **Avenida Michoacán** at **Parque México** and get off where you see the statue of a naked woman holding two jugs with water spilling into a fountain. There is a taxi sitio right in front of you where this tour will end. Avenida Mexico, the street that surrounds the park, would make a good walking tour by itself if your time is limited.

Meander through the park behind the amphitheater, passing by the duck pond. You will come upon a bridge and pond made of boulders with a geyser shooting water skyward. Turn right at the geyser and exit the park at the corner of Avenida Mexico and Sonora. Cross to the opposite corner and continue walking on Avenida México. In front of you will be the high-rise landmark **Edificio Basurto**, an art deco gem right out of a Fred Astaire movie. Try to get a peek at the lobby. Directly across from the Basurto is the trendy boutique **Hotel Hipodromo**.

At the next corner is **Plaza Popocatepetl**. Walk to your right around this circular park, whose side streets offer good examples of the architectural

mix of this area, with several restored art-deco gems. One block off the plaza on Calle Popocatepetl is **La Bodega**, a popular nightspot (p.99).
Continuing around the plaza, turn right at Calle Huichapan (also called Calle de Torreón) and you will see the traditional Mexican restaurant Flor de Lis, famous for its tamales.

At the next corner, turn left onto **Avenida Amsterdam,** and walk along its central pathway shaded by tall trees. This street was originally built as a racetrack, first for horses then later for automobiles, and so retains its oval shape; the official name for the area is Hipódromo.

Along Avenida Amsterdam, at the corner of Sonora, notice the pink Edificio San José with its playful tile work and fanciful rooftop structures. At Amsterdam #62 is the charming workshop of my local carpenter, Silvino.
At the next corner, Parras, is the Bistro Rojo, one of the better restaurants in the area, featuring a Mediterrenean-style menu.

Arriving at **Michoacán** (it intersects Amsterdam twice so it gets confusing) you will see an awning with the word **HOLA** ("hello") on it. This is one of the best taco stands in the city.

Featured in Saveur and other food magazines, it is known for its *tacos de guisados*, stewed concoctions served in a tortilla. There are several vegetarian options here, including cauliflower (*coliflor*), swiss chard (*acelgas*) and spinach (*espinacas*), and good *aguas frescas*, drinks made with tamarind (*tamarindo*) or hibiscus flowers (*jamaica*). If you are visiting in the morning or after dark, you can also find very good tamales sold in front of the Superama grocery store at the opposite corner.

At the next corner of Amsterdam, Ozulama, is a popular café which has an eclectic clientele—another good place for a break.

Continuing on Amsterdam you will reach **Plaza Citlaltepetl** with its simple central fountain. Just to your right there are two good places to eat, the homey El Bariloche, an Uruguyan restaurant with typical grilled meats and good pasta, and Foto Bistro, a former photography studio recently converted by its French owner into a trendy place with French-style bistro food and photographs lining the walls and serving excellent onion soup.
Walking in a loop, turn left at the Plaza, left again onto Calle Citlaltepetl, and left again onto

Calle Ozulama, noticing the tiled balconies and windows of the corner building.

Continue on Ozulama, past the café to the busy street Nuevo León. Cross over, heading toward the turquoise-painted El Péndulo, a café, book store and venue for live music on weekends (and clean bathrooms on the mezzanine).

Turn left at El Péndulo and walk one block along Saltillo, where the large blocky buildings create a Mondrian-like streetscape, then turn right on to Campeche, with its line of palm trees running down the middle.

When you reach Tamaulipas you will see El Tizoncito, home of the best tacos el pastor in town—rumor has it that they were invented here.

Cross Tamaulipas and continue along Campeche passing the Peluquería Excelsior, an old-style barber shop.

Turn right at Amatlán and walk one block to Michoacán. You are now on "restaurant row," the social center of La Condesa. The place is hopping, especially weekend nights, with beautiful, young Mexicans with lots of pesos to spend. It's a fun scene but most of the restaurants are all show with mediocre food. The best of the lot are Café Gloria and Fonda La Garufa. Avoid the truly awful Creperie de la Paix, even though it looks tempting.

At Amatlan #94 is Artefacto, a creative home design store.

(For a **gelato** break, turn left on Michoacán and walk two blocks (it's not Italy, but it's more than satisfying).)

From Amatlàn turn right on Michoacán where you encounter a 3-way intersection with Vicente Suarez and Atlixco. Cross this intersection to the left of the yellow market building (not a particularly interesting market) and turn left along Tamaulipas, which has even taller palms trees than Campeche. You will pass (yet another) Starbucks and a cluster of lively bars to reach Juan Escutia. Cross Juan Escutia and continue walking around the left side of **Parque España**, the slightly shabbier sibling of Parque Mexico just a few blocks away.

At the corner of Avenida Veracruz is the **Hotel Condesa DF**, with its ultra-trendy bar and restaurant.

If you are here around March and the jacaranda trees are in bloom, walk along Veracruz and be enchanted by millions of lavender-colored blossoms, or go up to the hotel's rooftop terrace. (At the far end of Veracruz are Metro Chapultepec and the entrance to the Parque Chapultepec.)

Walk through Parque España toward the far corner at Sonora. Cross the street toward the gas station and walk along Sonora two blocks until you reach Parque Mexico again. Turn right at the park (you are now on Avenida Mexico) and continue down to Michoacán, noticing the appealing architecture and tile details at #59 and #63. At the corner of Michoacán is one of my favorite buildings in the area, a modernist affair with the studio of my dreams on top. Just across the street you will find a taxi sitio next to the statue where this tour began, and where it ends. Go home and take a siesta.

If you want to pick up a bottle of wine and some bread and cheese before getting a cab, walk along Michoacán to the corner of Insurgentes to **La Naval**, in business for over 70 years. It has one of the best wine selections in town, as well as specialty foods and home-made breads.

OFF THE BEATEN TRACK IN LA CONDESA

Centro Cultural Bella Época (Tamaulipas 202 at Benjamin Hill). A large, well-stocked bookstore (lots of art and architecture books), gallery, café, cinema, and children's play area are housed in a smartly renovated Art Deco movie house.

Helados Roxy at the corner of Mazatlán and Montes de Oca, has been dishing out ice cream since the 1940's, and retains its old-fashioned charm.

Pasteleria la Gran Via (Amsterdam 288 near Sonora) Ask for their justly famous cream-filled merengues, which are guarded behind the counter.

Mukta Yoga (Amsterdam 171 at Plaza Citlaltepetl, tel. 5211-6036, www.muktayoga.com.mx) has drop-in yoga classes with great teachers.

Tianguis Most neighborhoods in Mexico City have a weekly street market known by the Aztec name tianguis. In Condesa there are tianguis on Tuesdays and Fridays which may remind you of street markets in Paris, without the cheese and the attitude. The produce is of high quality and is beautifully displayed; there are some good cooked food stalls, too (see p. 56).

The **Tuesday tianguis** is located on Calle Pachuca between Veracruz and Juan de la Barrera, not far from the Chapultepec metro station. Try the tacos de mixiote (shredded pork in a spicy red sauce) and empanadas de camarón (fried pastries with shrimp, avocado, onion, and cilantro). There are good quesadilla and tlacoyo vendors, too. My favorite tamales are here. Doña Marta sells tamales de mole and tamales Oaxaqueños (in a banana leaf) at the corner of Pachuca and Veracruz—she usually sells out by 11AM. There is a taxi sitio 2 blocks from the market at the corner of Augustin Melgar and José Vasconcelos

The **Friday tianguis** is at the corner of Nuevo León and Campeche. There is a nice old-fashioned neighborhood feel here, with baskets and pottery being sold along with fruits and vegetables, meat and fish. The prepared food stalls are great. You can find superior tacos de cecina adobada (pounded beef with chili) washed down with tepache, at one stand, and there's homemade torta de elote (sweet corn cake) avail-able next to that. You will also see people lining up for fresh blue corn quesadillas and tlacoyos.

The famous fountain in Parque México

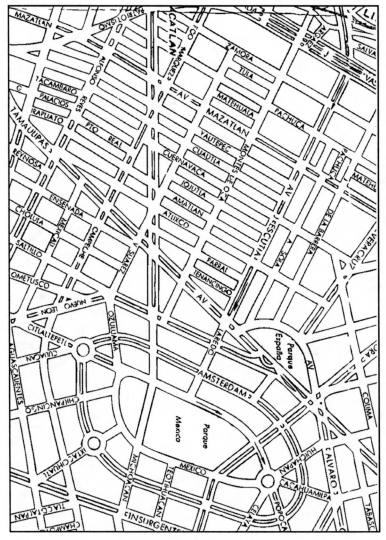

La Condesa

WALKING TOUR OF COLONIA ROMA

Colonia Roma was built in the early 20th century, the first fully planned residential neighborhood in the city. With its own electric, plumbing and street car lines it was considered the height of chic modernity and was the neighborhood of choice for many artists, writers, politicians, retired generals, and even a couple of bullfighters. Built during the last years of the dictatorship of Porfirio Diaz, who ruled Mexico from 1876 to 1910, it represents the French influence he helped promote all over the country (the ornate cast-iron kiosks found in the main squares of many Mexican towns date from this era). The original architecture features stone arches, balustrades, cornices and garlands, plus ornate iron-work and the occasional use of glazed tiles. Many of the old buildings are gone, replaced with a hodge-podge, but enough remains to give Colonia Roma its distinctive ambience. Here you can sense the Mexico City of another era, one that moved to the pace of horse and carriage. An innovative urban planning scheme placed mansions on the same blocks as humbler single-family homes and apartment buildings. This sense of a mixed neighborhood—rich and poor, traditional and modern, hip and dowdy— still prevails, and makes it interesting. There is a new energy in Roma after years of neglect and considerable damage from the 1985 earthquake, with a budding art gallery and café scene.

The nearest metro stops are Insurgentes (no. 1 line), and Hospital General (no. 3 line) but it is easier to begin the tour by taking a taxi to **Plaza Luís Cabrera** (at Zacatecas and Orizaba) in the heart of Colonia Roma. If you arrive in the morning you will find excellent tamales being sold by a street vendor here. Banana trees and fountains adorn this small park surrounded by cafés, restaurants and apartment buildings. Walk along the left side of the park toward Orizaba—be sure to notice the lovely house (#9) partially hidden by huge jacaranda trees. At Orizaba 139 stands one of the original mansions of the neighborhood, now a private university. The brick castle from 1910 at the next corner (Chihuhua) is another private home now used as a school. The Cafe d'Carlo and the Bella Italia ice cream store on the next block of Orizaba are two local favorites. The next intersection is Álvaro Obregón, the main thoroughfare of Colonia Roma. On the far right corner you will see **Casa Lamm**, another former mansion now transformed into the most important cultural center in the area, with a bookstore, galleries, art library, café and upscale restaurant with sliding glass walls that open to a small garden. This is the hottest spot in Roma, attracting the well-heeled and beautiful to its restaurant and art openings. It's worth a visit—be sure to go upstairs to see the original rooms with their elaborate molding and woodwork.

Go right as you leave Casa Lamm and walk down the camellon in the middle of Álvaro Obregón. This leafy walkway is marked by a series of classical bronze statues of naked men, a few iron benches, and a *bolero* eager to shine your shoes. It is especially nice in late afternoon as the sun cuts through the treetops and makes all the fountains sparkle. Shade and oxygen are provided by hundreds of ficus and rubber trees, eucalyptus, and especially the wax-leaf privet, whose simple blossoms, smelling of honeysuckle, perfume the air in the early months of summer.

Passing a statue of Satyr and Amor, you will see **Pasaje El Parian** on your left, an early version of a shopping mall, with quirky architectural detail. Most of the new shops inside sell clothing and accessories by young designers. Directly across the street is one of the ugliest buildings in Roma, the bulky blue Hospital Obregón, with a statue of Cantinflas, Mexico's beloved comic actor, out front.

Turn right at the next block, Jalapa, to explore the lovliest residential blocks in the neighborhood. You pass an old-time barber shop (Estetica Roma #99), The **Centro Budista de la Ciudad de México** (#94), and a beautiful blue residence (#92). Walk two blocks along Jalapa to Colima and turn left. Aside from a gap of modernity in the middle, this is the best preserved part of Roma. From Colima #226 to the corner of Tonalá (one of the few corners with all its original architecture intact) you can best imagine the life of Colonia Roma in its heyday. The ironwork on several houses here is especially noteworthy. On one corner (Tonalá 51) is the Museo Universitario de

Ciencias y Artes (MUCA) which shows contemporary art (when it is open).

Turn left on Tonalá and walk two blocks back to Alvaro Obregón, then left again two blocks which will bring you back to Casa Lamm, where this tour ends. There is a taxi sitio in front of Casa Lamm.

OFF THE TRACK IN ROMA

Chihuahua #78 (between Cordoba and Mérida) is the best example of Art Nouveau architecture in the city, recently restored.

Oskar's Uniform Store at the corner of Insurgentes and Guanajuato. This is one of my favorite surreal spots in the city. The oddly arranged mannequins will remind you of everything from "Night of the Living Dead" to Bernini's "Agony of Saint Teresa".

In the peaceful **Plaza Rio de Janeiro**, is a full-size replica of Michelangelos's David-no fig leaf here!

Casa Margolin (Cordoba #98 near Álvaro Obregón), has the best selection of classical music and music by Mexican composers in the city.

Mercado Medellín Colonia Roma has one of the better neighborhood markets, with good prepared food stalls. I go for lunch at one of the seafood places here. The market takes up a whole city block from Chiapas to Campeche, between Medellín and Monterrey.

Dulceria Celaya (Orizaba 37) is a branch of the original shop in the Centro selling traditional Mexican sweets.

Chic by Accident (Colima 180, near Jalapa), sells mid-20th century furniture originals and reproductions.

Antigüedades San Cristobal (Durango #87) You may feel like you are rummaging through a Mexican grandmother's attic at this store specializing exclusively in Mexican antiquities. (ring the bell if it looks closed.)

Pozolería Tizka (Zacatecas 59 between Merida and Cordoba) for delicious and inexpensive green pozole—one of my favorite foods in the city.

Massage If your feet are killing you, take a taxi to Medellin 151 (between Querètaro and San Luis

Potosì) for a reflexology foot massage with a machine. (30 pesos for half and hour).

Art Galleries...Mondays.

Some of the best for contemporary art in Roma are:

*   **Galería Nina Menocal**
    Zacatecas 93, (near Córdba)
*   **Galería OMR**
    at Plaza Rio de Janeiro where Orizaba and Durango intersect.
*   **Galería Florencia Riestra**,
    Colima 179 (near Jalapa)
*   **Galería Metropolitana**,
    Medellin 28 (near Sinaloa in Roma Norte)

art galleries Developers have been trying to promote Roma as the neighborhood of hip art galleries, and there are a few good ones—my favorites are listed below. At the galleries you can pick up a free monthly art map and guide (www.arte-mexico. com) with listings of what's showing all over town. Galleries in Mexico often have closed doors with buzzers or armed guards at the entry, making them very un-inviting, but don't let that put you off. Most galleries are closed on Sundays but open on Mondays.

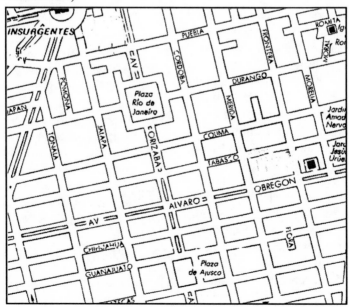

La Roma

OTHER INTERESTING COLONIAS

SANTA MARíA LA RIBERA

This working-class neighborhood near the Centro dates back to the mid-19th century, although much has been rebuilt. It has that distinctive Mexico City feel of simultaneous growth and decay. Artists are finding cheap places to live and work here, so there is a sense of expectation. Although few tourists visit, there are some worthwhile sights, and the very non-touristy nature of the place is what makes it appealing for a stroll. On the main plaza (called the Alameda) is a large cast-iron kiosk in Moorish style, built for the 1884 International Exposition in New Orleans, and later moved to this spot. On the west side of the plaza is the evocative **Museo de Geología**, which looks like an old movie set with its impressive woodwork, an elaborate cast-iron staircase and stained glass windows by José Maria Velasco, Mexico's renowned 19th century landscape painter; ask to go upstairs to see them. Diagonally across the plaza is a small restaurant run by a family of immigrants from Siberia if you are in the mood for blintzes or borscht. Near the museum, at the corner of Salvador Diaz Miron and J. Torres Bodet, is a classic old-style cantina, the **Salon Paris**. About 6 blocks away on Enrique González Martínez is the **Museo Universitario del Chopo**, the most impressive cast-iron structure of them all: you will see the twin spires towering over the neighborhood. Featured are changing exhibits of contemporary art, as well as a LGBT show during Gay pride month (June).

To get to this colonia, take a taxi to the Alameda de Santa Maria la Ribera, or take the metrobus north on Insurgentes to the Buenavista stop, go right 3 blocks on Jose Alzate, then turn right on Dr. Atl and walk one block to the Alameda.

The nearby **Museo de San Carlos**, (Avenida Puente de Alvarado 50—one of the only museums open on Mondays) makes a good addition to a tour of this area. It is housed in a lovely former mansion, with a small but classy collection of European art, including several works by Zurburán and a quirky Pontormo. There is a quiet café in back.

ZONA ROSA

This area is often thought of as an important tourist destination, but it is of limited interest to me.

From the 1940's through the 1960's it was the glamorous residential and nightlife area of the city, but it has gotten a bit tacky over the years. Many international restaurants, hotels and stores will make you feel like you are still at home. It is, however, the center of gay social life—check out **calle Amberes** (near Reforma) with its cafés, restaurants and bars. There is also a weekend flea market at the Plaza del Angel (between Hamburgo and Londres near Amberes) with some high-end antiques. The nearest metro stop is Insurgentes on the #1 line.

El Kiosko Moro, Santa Maria de la Ribera

POLANCO

This neighborhood, first developed in the late 1930's, is one of the most desirable residential areas in the city, with lots of fancy shops, good restaurants, embassies, galleries, tree-lined streets and parks. It is home to a sizeable Jewish community, as well as foreigners working in big business and the embassies. Avenida Presidente Masaryk is the Rodeo Drive or Fifth Avenue of Mexico City, with all the big name stores—Gucci, Pucci, Hermes, etc. The **Centro Commercial Moliere** (Moliere and Horacio) is a beautifully designed, upscale mall. Appealing old houses in 'Hollywood Mexican' style (with elaborate carved decorations) and curious topiaries on some residential streets give Polanco a certain style, but it is mixed with a lot of standard steel-and-glass boxy stuff. Polanco is spread out and not ideal for walking, but if you want to get a feel for the neighborhood, take a taxi to the corner of Julio Verne and Emilio Castelar (there is a taxi sitio here for your return trip). The streets radiating from this point comprise the closest thing to a center of Polanco, with lots of restaurants and shops, and 50's–style apartment buildings with rounded corners.

Polanco is home to most of the city's "blue chip" art venues. Look for the free art map at any of these galleries.

Worth visiting are:

• **Galería Lopez Quiroga** (Aristóteles 169 at Horacio) represents some of the best Mexican abstract artists. (www.lopezquiroga.com)

• **Galería Mexicana de Diseño** (Anatole France 13). Furniture and objects for the home by young Mexican designers are shown here.

• **Galería Praxis** (Arquimedes 175) This gallery specializes in Latin American realist painting. (www.praxismexico.com)

• **Galería Enrique Guerrero** (Horacio 1549-A). Shows some big names in contemporary art (www.galeriaenriqueguerrero.com)

• **Museo Sala de Arte Publico David Alfaro Siqueiros** (Trés Picos 29). Siqueiros donated his home to the Mexican government as a museum in 1974. A permanent collection about his life and work is supplemented by temporary exhibits of contemporary artists.

The nearest metro stop is Polanco on the #7 line.

XOCHIMILCO

At the southern edge of the city (about 20 km. from the Centro) is the village of Xochimilco, now absorbed into the metropolitan area. You can happily spend a full day here visiting three main attractions: the Museo Dolores Olmedo, the market, and the so-called Floating Gardens. The gardens refer to *chinampas*, which date back to pre-Aztec times. These are small islands created by enclosing an area of the lake with a basketry fence, then rooting plants within the perimeter and mounding compost on top to create highly fertile planting grounds. Plant and flower growers live and work here, as they have for centuries. Colorful wooden pole-boats called *trajineras* can be rented to glide through the network of canals created by the chinampas. On weekends there is a festive atmosphere as hundreds of families take to the canals, along with floating mariachis, food and drink vendors, and souvenir sellers. During the week it is much quieter, although still lively—it is when I prefer to visit. Sundays are most crowded. Look for the classic Mexican movie, *Maria Candelaria* from 1944 with Dolores Del Rio as an Indian flower seller to see wonderfully romantic images of the Xochimilco of yesteryear.

Museo Dolores Olmedo Patiño (Avenida Mexico 5843, tel. 5555-0891). This is one of my favorite museums anywhere, great art in a beautiful setting. Dolores Olmedo, a rich socialite patron of Diego Rivera, opened her house and collection to the public in 1994. Wandering through the beautifully landscaped grounds with strutting peacocks and waddling ducks, you arrive at the 16th century hacienda. Out front is a fenced-off area where several xoloitzcuintzles, rare hairless dogs of pre-hispanic origin, are frolicking or sleeping. The ceramic sculptures of these dogs from the state of Colima are a highlight of the museum's small but impressive pre-Colombian collection. A good sampling of works by **Diego Rivera** is here, including a roomful of luscious small paintings of sunsets and some excellent lithographs. **Frida Kahlo** has her own room, the single largest collection of her work and far better than what you will find in Frida's own house in Coyoacán. At the end is an exhibit of Mexican handicrafts, also of high quality and a pleasant outdoor snack bar. The peacocks wander freely here—more than once I have been within a few feet of a full-feather display.

After opening her museum, Olmedo continued to live on the property until her death in 2002. Her private quarters are now open to the public, a garish display of wealth with too many Chinese antiques and too many photos of herself looking rich and imperious.

See the website (www. museodoloresolmedo.org) for more information and a map to get there—make a copy for your taxi driver if going by cab as almost everyone has trouble finding this place.

Getting There: Many hotels offer tours of Xochimilco by taxi or minivan, or you can engage a taxi by the hour at any sitio. You can also reach the museum by metro. Take the #2 line to the last stop, Tasqueña, then switch to the *tren ligero*, an above-ground extension of the metro (you will need to buy a separate ticket). Get off at La Noria station and make a U-turn when you reach the green pedestrian overpass (you will be on the Antiguo Camino a Xochimilco). The museum is one block down the street across from the Pemex gas station.

You can hail a cab in front of the museum or walk back to the pedestrian overpass, where you will find a taxi sitio across the street on the left (tel. 5676-0409). Or take any of the small green buses marked Xochimilco which go along Avenida Guadalupe Ramirez to the center of town, about a mile away. You will know when to get off when you see the white dome of the church ahead of you. Flanking the entrance to the church are the two halves of the town plaza. On the left is Jardín Juarez with its gazebo, gardens and benches. On the right is Jardín Morelos which has been given over to vendors, many selling CD's and DVD's. The cacophony here is most impressive. The bustling Mercado de Xochimilco is just behind the row of tall palm trees.

The **market** consists of two buildings, both marked with tall Mi Mercado signs. The one facing the plaza is marked Xochitl Zona and contains mostly fruits, vegetables and meats, with a few good pottery stalls outside. The other building, Xochimilco Anexo, is just behind the first. Here you will find plants, flowers and several small fondas serving inexpensive Mexican food. Both are classic examples of neighborhood Mexican markets, lively and colorful. Between the two market buildings on the right (Calle Morales) is the lovely El Rosario church, a little gem perfect for a moment of tranquility.

Floating gardens From the market you can walk or take a pedicab to several nearby *embarcaderos* (boat landings) where you can rent a boat for a canal ride. Young men may solicit you to accompany them to a specific embarcadero and will help you arrange a boat rental—this may seem creepy at first, but don't worry, they are just doing their job. They are paid a small commission by the boat owner. Prices for boats are posted and will vary depending on the size of the boat and the length of the tour (one hour minimum)—be sure to agree on the total price before you set out. A small tip for the boatman is customary.

If you need a taxi there is a sitio on Calle Miguel Hidalgo near Pino, not far from the Jardín Juarez. It is slightly obscured by street vendors—look for it near the entrance of the Bodega Commercial Mexicana.

A vendor in the canals of Xochimilco

OTHER PLACES AND EVENTS OF INTEREST AROUND THE CITY

Teotihuacán About 35 miles NE of the city are the remains of the ancient civilization of Teotihuacán, one of the most impressive sites of a vanished culture anywhere in the world. The city flourished from about 100 to 750 A.D. with population estimates as high as 200,000. By the time the Aztecs arrived in the area, it had been abandonded for 700 years, although they cleverly appropriated its history as their own, claiming it as the birth and burial place of their gods. The broad, serene spaces and the simple grandeur of the architecture give the site an awe-inspiring power. The so-called Pyramid of the Sun is the 3rd largest pyramid in the world, after Cholula in Mexico and Cheops in Egypt. There are some interesting carved details and fragments of painted murals in situ, and two separate museums, one of artifacts, one of mural painting (I find the exhibits in the Museo de Antropología even better, however.) The Palacio de Quetzalpapálotl has the most interesting interior spaces. Maps, guide books, and all kinds of tacky souvenirs are available as you enter the ruins.

Plan at least 6 hours for a visit, including transportation time. Sitio and hotel taxis will take you for a hefty price (starting around US$80), but you can also go by bus from Terminal Norte for about US$6 per person, round trip. Autobuses Teotihuacán leave every 15 to 30 minutes (starting at 7AM) from the far end of the bus station, near Sala 8. The last bus leaves the ruins at 6PM. Bring a hat, water and sunscreen as there is no shade at all at the ruins and you will walk several miles to cover the entire area. There are many restaurants on the road circling the ruins—an interesting choice is La Gruta, located in a cool cave by Puerta 5.

There is a hotel near the ruins (www.teotihuacaninfo.com). You might consider staying your last night there and visit the ruins in early morning when it is cooler and the tour buses have not arrived. The hotel can arrange transportation to the airport.

On January 1 and the spring and summer solstices, thousands flock to the ruins, so be aware that traffic may be horrendous on those days.

Casa/Estudio Luís Barragán General Francisco Ramírez no.

14, Colonia Tacubaya. Call for appointment, 5515-4908.) Mexico's important and influential architect Luis Barragán (1902–1988) combined elements of modernism with traditional Mexican materials. A visit to his home and studio, which was named a UNESCO World Heritage Site in 2004, is a sublime and mystical architectural experience. Taxis might have a hard time finding this place, so bring a map, or take the metro #7 to Constituyentes and follow the sidewalk alongside the traffic on Avenida Constituyentes one block to Francisco Ramírez.

Casa de la Bola (Parque Lira 136, Colonia Tacubaya, near Metro Tacubaya on the #1 or #7 line) This colonial mansion redone in sumptuous 19th—century style is one of the hidden gems of the city, a good place to dream of times past and for a moment of tranquility strolling through adjacent Parque Lira. It is open only on Sunday from 11 to 5, or by appointment (call 5515-5582)

Secretaría de Comunicaciones y Transportes
(Avenida Xola near Eje Central, the nearest metro is Etiopia on the #3 line, then take a pesero). This architectural complex of govern-

ment office buildings, which dates from 1953, was severely damaged in the 1985 earthquake, but has since been repaired. The mosaic stone murals depicting episodes from Mexican history, of epic proportions, are justly famous. Be sure to check out the heroic figurative sculptures adorning the entryway.

Basilica de la Virgen de Guadalupe
Mexico is 90% Catholic and there is no more powerful image for Mexican Catholics than La Virgen de Guadalupe. She is so beloved that both boys and girls are named after her and millions of pilgrims visit her each year, some crawling the last miles on hands and knees. The Basilica looks like a Las Vegas night club and the miraculous shroud is viewed from a conveyor belt, but nearby the awkwardly tilting Colegiata and the tile-crowned El Pocito church are beautiful colonial era buildings worth noting. More than the sights however, it is the ambience, equally fervent and festive, that makes this place worth visiting. You can take the metrobus north on Insurgentes to Deportivo 18 de Marzo, then walk about 5 blocks west. You will see the top of the Basilica from the bridge as you exit the station. You can also arrive by

metro, La Villa-Basilica station on the no. 6 line.

Centro Nacional de las Artes (CENART) (Rio Churubusco at Tlalpan, metro Ermita on the #2 line). Anyone interested in modern architecture will love taking a stroll through this campus, where you can see buildings by several of Mexico's prominent late 20th-century architects. It is the most important art school in the country, with faculties in painting, sculpture, cinema, music, and dance. Look for frequent concert and dance events listed in Tiempo Libre magazine.

La Colección Jumex The most important private collection of contemporary art is located north of the city in the industrial zone of Ecatapec. Jumex is Mexico's largest producer of bottled fruit juices, and its heir, Eugenio Lopez Alonso, has created an impressive collection housed within the factory confines in beautiful gallery spaces. Call for information and directions 5775-8188 (www.lacoleccionjumex.org)

Galeria de Arte Mexicano (Gobernador Rafael Rebollar 43 Col. San Miguel Chapultepec, in the same neighborhood as the Casa/Estudio Luís Barragán Tel. 5273-1261) Founded in 1935, this was the city's first gallery, showing amongst others Frida Kahlo and Diego Rivera. They now mix well known artists with promising newcomers.

THE BEST MUSEUMS
IN MEXICO CITY

- Museo de Antropología   p.38
- Museo de Arte Popular   p.26
- Museo Dolores Olmedo Patiño   p.71
- Museo Franz Mayer   p.26
- Museo Nacional de Arte   p.36
- Museo de Bellas Artes   p.25
- Museo de Arte Moderno   p. 55
- Museo Rufino Tamayo   p.40
- Museo de San Carlos   p.68
- Museo Diego Rivera (Anahuacalli)   p.50
- Museo-Estudio Diego Rivera y Frida Kahlo   p.53
- Museo Mural Diego Rivera   p.27
- Museo Frida Kahlo   p.49
- Museo Carrillo Gil   p.53
- Museo de la Estampa   p.26
- Museo de la Ciudad de Mexico   p.36
- Museo Leon Trotsky   p.50
- Museo de Geología   p.68
- Museo del Carmen   p.52
- Museo SCHP (Arzobispado)   p.31
- Museo del Universitario del Chopo   p.68
- Laboratorio Arte Alameda   p.27
- Sala de Arte Público Siqueiros   p.70
- Casa/Estudio Luís Barragán   p.74

FOOD
WHAT AND WHERE TO EAT

Mexico's culinary history dates back to Aztec times and includes influences from Spanish, French and Lebanese immigrants, among others. Corn, tomatoes, potatoes, avocados, chilies, turkey, chocolate and vanilla were first encountered in the New World, and they remain fundamental to Mexican cooking. The quality of fruits, vegetables, meat and fish is high. Plastic-wrapped, pre-cooked or highly processed food is not the norm here, so basic ingredients have real flavor. Mexico City is a great food town. Here are some of my favorite things and where to find them.

The following is a brief list of some of the most common and popular foods you will encounter in Mexico City. Try them all.

Tortillas The staff of life of Mexican cuisine, the ubiquitous tortilla is essentially ground corn flattened into a 6-inch disc and cooked on a dry griddle (tortillas are sometimes made of wheat, more common in the north.) Millions are eaten daily—and have been for centuries. They are the basic ingredient for tacos, enchiladas, tostadas, burritos, chilaquiles, flautas, and a host of other Mexican dishes. Fried tortilla chips, served as a snack or appetizer, are called *totopos*.

Antojitos This is a food category, not a dish, but you will see the word a lot. Its meaning, literally "before the eyes", can vary, but it most often refers to corn-based appetizers, anything made with tortillas or masa de maíz (corn dough). They are eaten as a light meal or snack (although they can often be quite filling). Like Italian pasta, a basic ingredient appears in a variety of shapes and sizes. Some of the most common antojitos found in Mexico City are quesadillas, tlacoyos, gorditas, sopes, panuchos, tacos, tamales, huaraches, and enchiladas.

Tamales Don't leave Mexico without eating a tamal (singular form of the word in Spanish), even if you think you know them from other places. Millions are eaten daily and have been since before the Aztecs arrived. They are delicious and comforting. Tamales vary from region to region, but the basic idea is ground corn wrapped in its husk (usually corn) and steamed for hours. The *masa* (corn dough) is mixed with lard and usually contains a small amount of filling: chicken or pork with red sauce, green sauce, or mole, or strips of chile poblano with cheese are the most common. Tamales Oaxaqueños are wrapped in banana leaves and have a smoother texture. The filling is really only a flavoring—the main event is the corn itself, its flavor and texture. Discard the corn husk or banana leaf. Tamales are usually eaten in the morning and at night. In residential zones, market areas, outside metro stations, and around the Zócalo, you will see street corner vendors tending large shiny steel containers with steam escaping from the edges. Because tamales cook for many hours and are sold hot, they are a hygenic street food.

The best tamales I have eaten have been from street vendors but you can find them in some restaurants, too, especially on breakfast menus. They are a specialty of **Flor de Lis** in Colonia Condesa. Each year around Candelaria, on February 2nd, there is a *Festival* *de* Tamales at the cultural center of Coyoacán that is worth the trip—tamales from all over Latin America are sold. Along with tamales, Mexicans often drink atole, a thick, hot drink made of finely ground corn, sometimes rice, and usually flavored with fruit (guayaba is a favorite), chocolate, vanilla or even coffee. I am not a big fan of the drink—for me it is too rich to have with tamales—but my friend Kathy swears it is a cure for menstrual cramps, and it is very comforting on a cold winter morning.

Tamal vendor in the
Condesa tianguis

Tacos The crispy things with ground beef, cheddar cheese and lettuce that are sold as tacos in the U.S. are not found in Mexico. A taco here is a soft corn tortilla with a small amount of filling, rolled up and eaten with your hands. When a wheat tortilla is used, it is called a burrito. Tacos are found everywhere, eaten day and night, and they can be considered essential to most Mexican diets. Meat is the preferred filling, but vegetable and seafood can be found. Most popular are *carnitas* (chopped roast pork), *barbacoa* (pit-cooked sheep or goat), *chicharrón* (pork rind), but you can also find tacos made of eyes, ears, nose and brain. My favorite is *tacos al pastor*, which reflect Arab influence in Mexican cuisine: small slices of seasoned pork are cut from a rotating spindle (you will notice them all over town) and served with a bit of pineapple, chopped onion and cilantro. A good *taquería* will have an alluring selection of salsas to spice things up. The other major category is *tacos de guisado*, cooked or stewed fillings, often with vegetables.

Tlacoyos This common antojito, both satisfying and delicious, is found on street corners and near markets throughout the city. Almost always made by women

THE BEST TACO JOINTS IN TOWN

Tacos Beatriz, (Uruguay 30, near Bolivar) This funky institution in the Centro, supposedly the oldest taquería opened 1907, serves tacos de guisados and *tepache*, a lightly fermented drink made from pineapple juice. Their mole is excellent.

Salón la Corona (Bolivar 24, Centro). This belly-up-to-the-bar kind of place has been feeding happy taco eaters since 1928. The bacalao (dried salt cod) and mole verde are especially good.

El Tizoncito (at the corner of Tamaulipas and Nuevo León, Condesa) This place claims to be the originator of tacos al pastor, *¿quien sabe?* But they are excellent and their salsas are too.

El Güero (Avenida Amsterdam 135 near Michoacán, Condesa) These are my favorite *tacos de guisado,* with several vegetarian choices: try the cooked leafy greens *quelites* or *acelgas* (swiss chard) or *coliflór* (fried cauliflower.) This hole-in-the-wall has appeared in Saveur magazine.

Tacos Alvaro O. (Alvaro Obregón 90 near Orizaba, Roma), for classic grilled meat tacos

El Jarocho (at the corner of Manzanillo and Tapachula, Colonia Roma). The *tacos de guisado* here although pricey, are huge; they have been in business for over 50 years.

El Rincòn de la Lechuza (Miguel Angel Quevedo 34 at Insurgentes, Coyoacán) My friend Rachel and her kids claim these are the best tacos al pastor in the city.

sitting on the ground with a *comal* (or clay plate), this wonderful food was probably eaten by the Aztecs in much the same form. Blue or yellow corn masa (dough) is formed by hand into a small lozenge, flattened, and filled with cheese (requesón) or fava beans (habas, my favorite), then cooked on a dry griddle. When done, it is topped with chopped nopales, onions, cilantro, queso fresco and red or green salsa. Tlacoyos, considered common street food, are rarely found in restaurants. My favorite place to eat them is in front of the Museo de la Estampa behind the Palacio de Bellas Artes, but you will find them all over town.

Quesadillas Often found with tlacoyos at street stalls. Most commonly, a large corn tortilla is filled, folded and cooked on a round metal griddle. Sometimes they are deep-fried, but I usually avoid these on the street. There are many kinds of fillings, my favorites are flor de calabaza (cheese and squash blossom flowers), huitlacoche (a corn fungus with a mushroom-like taste), and quelites (a spinach-like green). Excellent deep-fried quesadillas are found in the market in Coyoacán—not on anyone's diet, but worth the calories.

Sopes Small discs of corn masa are fried and then topped with beans, chicken, chorizo sausage—the variety is endless. These are often served as appetizers in restaurants or at street stalls.

Gorditas Pockets of corn masa are cooked on a griddle and stuffed with beans, meat, nopales, etc. This is one of the most common street foods in Mexico City.

Tortas Mexico´s version of the sandwich generally fills a *bolillo*, or soft roll, with a wide range of ingredients. A few popular choices are *milanesa* (pounded and fried meat), *pierna* (roast pork), and *choriqueso* (cheese and sausage), but the variety is endless. Garnishes include tomato, onion, avocado, cheese, lettuce, mayonaise, and of course, chile jalapeño or chipotle.

Mole (pronounced MO-lay) is a thick, complex sauce usually served with chicken, and there are as many variations as there are cooks. The term "mas Mexicano que mole" is like saying "as American as apple pie"—it is considered by many to be the national dish. Mole was supposedly invented by nuns in a convent in Puebla who wanted to impress a visiting bishop by creating a new sauce that combined ingredients from both Europe and Mexico. Most mole recipes contain dried chillies, herbs, ground seeds or nuts, tomatoes, and often a bit of chocolate. The moles most frequently found in Mexico City are *rojo* (which really looks dark brown), *negro* (from Oaxaca) and *verde*, which has no chocolate. Mole is most often served with a piece of chicken or as enchiladas (sometimes called enmoladas). Most restaurants that serve Mexican food will have some form of mole on their menu. My

Quesadilla and Sope stand in La Lagunilla flea market

favorite moles are in two very humble places: **Tacos Beatriz** (see p.81) and **Fonda Mi Lupita,** (Buentono 22, near Salto de Agua metro, and not far from the Mercado San Juan) which has been serving mole poblano since 1957. Their enchiladas de mole are served with the traditional garnish of raw onion rings, sesame seeds and crumbled *queso fresco* or fresh white cheese.

Sopas You can always count on good, homemade soup in Mexican restaurants. *Consomé de Pollo* or *Caldo de Pollo* is chicken soup but usually comes with lots of chicken and vegetables—order this if your stomach needs a rest. My favorite soups are *Sopa de Tortilla* or *Sopa Azteca*, made with chicken broth, tomatoes, chilies, crisp tortilla strips, avocado and cheese. *Sopa de Flor de Calabaza*, made with squash blossoms, and *Sopa de Ajo,* garlic soup are also traditional favorites.

Pozole A thick satisfying soup, almost a stew, with pre-hispanic roots. Red pozole, the most common, has a pork and tomato base, contains large corn kernels (hominy), and is served with radish, lettuce, onion and oregano which you add according to taste. There is a very good pozole stand on the street in front of Calle San Ildefonso #42 in the Centro and inside the Mercado San Juan on weekends. Pozole Verde can be found at **Pozoleria Tizka** (Calle Zacatecas 59, between Cordoba and Merida in Colonia Roma). I used to live upstairs from this place, so I ate here a lot. It remains one of my favorite foods in Mexico, and I haven't found it anywhere else. Ground pumpkin seeds provide the thick green soup base. I order it with shredded chicken instead of pork. Their tostadas (fried tortillas) are the best I have eaten. Wash it all down with their refreshing lemonade. Good pozole is also found in the Xochimilco market, the Mercado de Antojitos in Coyoacán, and on Saturdays only, at Doña Juana´s stand in the Mercado San Juan.

Nopales Cactus paddles are eaten as a vegetable throughout Mexico and are food of the poorest Mexicans. You will see them at most taco and tlacoyo stands. *Ensalada de nopales* (cactus salad with onions, cilantro, and tomato), which you will find on many menus, is a good way to try them. They have a mild, slightly acidic green bean-like flavor, and, if not cooked properly, can emit a slimy liquid like okra.

Guacamole Most visitors to Mexico will know this avocado concoction, which has many variations, but be sure to try it here and find out what real avocados taste like.

Chiles en Nogada This classic Mexican dish is popular around *Fiestas Patrias* (Independence Day in September), but is served year-round in some restaurants. Green poblano chilies are filled with a mixture of ground meat and raisins or other dried fruit, topped with a white sauce made of ground pecans and cream and sprinkled with pomegranate seeds. It is usually served at room temperature. The three colors represent the Mexican flag.

Frutas Mexico has some exotic fruits you might not find back home, so be sure to sample them. Fresh, ripe fruit is easy to come by and you will probably see papaya and melón (cantaloupe) on most breakfast menus. Plátanos (bananas) are exceptionally flavorful in Mexico. The very little ones, called dominicos, are my favorite. You may notice zapotes in the market. About the size of an orange with thin green skin and black flesh, they are sold ripe and look like they are about to fall apart. It is sometimes served as a dessert, pureed with

orange juice and tequila, or as an ice cream flavor. You will see mangos sold on sticks with chili and lime by street vendors in Parque Chapultapec. If you are here during mango season (summer months) when they are very sweet and juicy, be sure to try one. I buy them at the market, peel the skin with a knife and stand over the sink to eat them. The familiar big magenta ones sold for export are the least tasty, and more likely to be stringy. The smaller, lime-green ones (sometimes called manilas) are best. Pitahayas can be seen in paintings by Frida Kahlo, who was drawn to their exotic appearance, and found in better markets. They look like small hot-pink footballs with tiny fins, with a bluish flesh flecked with tiny black seeds. The flavor is similar to kiwi, but milder. Red and green tunas are cactus fruits best enoyed as a drink (they have lots of tiny black seeds that need to be strained) Ping-pong ball sized yellow guayabas are fragrant fruits also best in drinks because of their seeds—try a *licuado de platano y guayaba*.

Aguas Frescas literally "fresh waters", these are traditional drinks made with fresh fruits and vegetables (among other ingredients) pureed in a blender with sugar and water. They are found in most Mexican restaurants and food stalls, although sometimes you won't see them on the menu, so be sure to ask. The most common flavors are *jamaica* (hibiscus flower), *tamarindo* (pulp from tamarind seeds) and horchata which is made from rice, sometimes almonds; there is no milk in this white drink. A host of fruits: mango, papaya, watermelon and cantaloupe are also used.

Plain purified drinking water is called *agua natural*; if you just ask for *agua* in some places you might be served *agua fresca*.

Jugos You will notice fresh fruit juices at street stalls throughout the city, lined up in a colorful display. Orange, carrot, and beet are the most common. Try a *vampiro* which includes all three and sometimes celery, too. Do not drink pure beet juice—it wreaks havoc on your stomach. **Jugos Canadá** (see Walking Tour of Centro Historico #1) is a great place to go for all kinds of juices. On the other side of the Zócalo (Pino Suarez 18) is the tiny **Jugería Maria Cristina,** where they have been serving juice drinks since 1944.

Limonada Lemonade is available everywhere in Mexico and is delicious and refreshing. Made with small green limes called *limones*, it is mixed with either plain water (*agua natural*) or sparkling water (*agua mineral*).

Tequila Mexico's most famous alcohol is made from the heart of the agave cactus. Many foreigners only drink it mixed as a margarita, but few Mexicans order it that way. If you want to appear more like a native, order *"un tequila"* (not *"una" tequila*) with *sangrita:* literally "little blood". You will be served two small glasses, one with straight tequila and one with a spicy red drink made of tomato juice with various additions, usually pomegranate or orange juice and hot sauce. Alternate sips from the two glasses.

There are three basic types of tequila: *blanco, reposado*, and *añejo*. Reposados are aged and usually amber colored and tend to be more expensive, but some people prefer the stronger bite of the clear blancos; it is purely a matter of personal taste. Añejos have been aged longer and tend to be smoother. Most bars have good selections which waiters can explain, but be sure to check prices as some get very expensive, especially if the waiter seems to be pushing his choice.

Mezcal is a variation of tequila, made from agave as well as other cactus plants. Most of it comes from the state of Oaxaca. It usually has a smoky, almost charcoal-like taste, and in my experience, packs a stronger wallop than tequila.

Pulque is made by fermenting (not distilling) the sap of the maguey cactus. It has a thick texture and a yeasty taste. *Curados* are pulques that have been flavored with fruits, vegetables or nuts. Pulque was used in Aztec rituals and has a long association as a drink of the common man. It is usually served only in pulquerias which are slowly disappearing. You can find it at **La Hortensia** in Plaza Garibaldi, and also at **Las Duelistas** (Aranda 30 near Ayuntamiento, Centro), a funky place that's been around for 50 years, featuring curados of celery, beet, and other exotic flavors. Unaccompanied women may attract unwanted attention in these places: beware.

Postres Mexico is not famous for its desserts but there are a few classics I recommend. Flan (egg custard) is served everywhere, but avoid the too-yellow, rubbery kind often served with an inexpensive comida corrida. Pastel de Tres Leches is a rich layer cake made with whole milk, evaporated milk and sweetened condensed milk. Pay de limón (lemon

pie) and pay de nuez (pecan pie) are favorites you will find on many menus. Chongos are odd-looking curds of sweet milk in sugar syrup that might startle at first but become addictive. Mexican bakeries (pastelerias) offer lots of tempting cakes and cookies. In most places you pick up a metal tray and tongs, serve yourself and head to the cashier. Although the variety of shapes, sizes and colors is impressive, you will find that most of it tastes pretty much the same.

Chocolate Aztecs mixed cocoa with chili and drank it for festive occasions, introducing its use to the rest of the world. Today, the best way to try Mexican chocolate is mixed with hot milk and served with churros, a sweet fried dough stick. **Churros y Chocolate 'El Moro'** (Eje Central 42 near Uruguay, Centro) has been around since 1935 and is open 24 hour a day. It's a good stop after a performance at Bellas Artes. Hexagonal boxes of Abuela or Ibarra brands of chocolate, available at any grocery store, make nice gifts. (Break up tablets of chocolate and mix in a blender with hot milk.) Chocolate candy and desserts, on the other hand, are often disappointing, even though they might look great. I love chocolate and have eaten many mediocre chocolate desserts in search of the truly delicious. Sanborn's, that wonderful chain of restaurant/stores that always seems to come in handy, sells chocolates by weight—100 grams is a good amount to start with. Of the many choices a few are really good. I recommend maronet amargo, avellaneda, hojas de cassis, tortugas,and the almendras.

Comida Corrida You will see these words all over town in fondas and comedores, simple eateries that cater to working class Mexicans looking for an economic home-cooked meal. A complete meal consisting of soup, rice, main course and often dessert and beverage can be had for a few dollars. Sometimes the food is bland and watery, but you can also find hearty and delicious meals and get the experience of how the people eat. Look for places that are clean and busy.

WHERE TO EAT

Here are my favorites (more recommendations are found in the Walking Tours)

DESAYUNO (Breakfast).

Mexicans love a big breakfast. You might see someone eating half a chicken or a big steak at 8 AM. *Huevos a la Mexicana* (scrambled eggs with pepper, tomato and onion) or *Huevos Rancheros* (fried egg on a tortilla with salsa roja) are among the many ways eggs are prepared in Mexico. *Chilaquiles*, which make use of yesterday's tortillas by frying them up with salsa, then adding *crema* (Mexico's delicious version of *crème fraiche*) and onions, is a favorite comfort food.

Hotel Majestic (on the Zócalo at Cinco de Mayo) The rooftop restaurant, with its spectacular view, is a great place to start a tour of the Zócalo.

Sanborn's (Casa de los Azulejos, Madero 4, Centro). The central patio in this former colonial mansion is another picturesque spot, best at breakfast. Open 7 AM–1 AM.

Bisquet's is a chain of restaurants with various locations, famous for their cafe con leche. It is poured from two steaming pitchers, one for milk, and the other for a dense coffee concentrate. Most Mexicans drink it very light, but I find a 50–50 mixture best. There are Bisquet's in the Centro at Tacuba 85 and Madero 29, and in Colonia Roma (Álvaro Obregon at Merida).

Teka'fe (Motolinia 31-A) This cozy spot on a pedestrian street in the Centro has been around for decades, with only the addition of a TV to break the mood.

Casa Lamm (Álvaro Obregon at Orizaba) is an elegant place to have breakfast before starting the Walking Tour of Colonia Roma.

Maque (Ozulama and Avenida Mexico). Start a tour of Colonia Condesa with breakfast at this popular outdoor café near Parque Mexico. Although a bit pricey, their menu is a glossary of Mexican breakfast foods, and the homemade pastry is good, too.

COMIDA (Lunch). This is

the main meal of the day for most Mexicans and is usually not eaten before 2 PM, often lasting for hours. Mexicans love to *sobremesar*, sit around and chat after eating. The American idea of eating, paying and leaving seems strange to Mexicans, and it **is** considered rude to be handed the check without asking for it. You will see simple, home-style comida corrida restaurants all over town, offering set meals at low prices for the hordes of city workers who can't get home for lunchtime. Meals are cheap and filling, and in the best places, delicious.

Puro Corazón (Monte de Piedad 11, west side of the Zócalo, 5518-0300), Atop a 6-story building that houses a gallery and store of Mexican artesanias, this place has the best views of the Zócalo. Open from 8am to 8pm every day. The menu features Mexican food that is well prepared and reasonably priced for such a prime location. The tortas de huazontle are an unusual treat.

Danubio (Uruguay 3, tel. 5512-0912, Centro). This beloved institution, around since the 1930's, is famous for seafood, but the once charming decor has been somewhat altered. I find much of the food dull, but the camarones al ajillo (shrimp with garlic and chili cooked in sizzling oil) is superior—a must for garlic lovers.

Coox Hanal (Isabel la Católica 83 near Mesones, upstairs, Centro). This is the best place for Yucatecan cuisine. Several of my friends had their favorite meal in Mexico City here. Try the panuchos (tortillas with black beans and cochinita pibil, a spicy shredded pork), papadzules (tortillas rolled up with chopped eggs and a green pumpkin seed sauce—a good choice for *vegetrians*), pan de cazón (tortilla and shark), sopa de lima (chicken soup perfumed with special limes), and horchata (a sweet drink made of rice). Inexpensive, no reservations, open from 10:30 to 6:30. There is a swing set on the roof for the kids.

Café del Palacio Located in the lobby of the Palacio de Bellas Artes, this is a pleasant place to eat and the prices are reasonable. The international menu has sandwiches, salads, as well as heftier fare.

La Gran Cocina Mi Fonda (Lopez 101, Centro) This humble but charming eatery serves its regular customers home-cooked Spanish food with a Mexican touch—the perfect roast chicken. A full meal costs no more than US$4—the decor and prices unchanged since 1950.

Contramar (Calle Durango 200, near Plaza Cybelles in Colonia Roma, 5514-3169). Open for lunch only, this fashionable spot is one of the best seafood restaurants in town, with a fun, bright atmosphere. The tuna sashimi and the pescado a la talla, cooked with 2 salsas–half red, half green, are special Reservations are necessary.

El Bajio (Avenida Cuitláhuac 2709, tel. 5341-9889, Colonia Azcapotzalco, Metro Cuitláhuac on the #2 line). You might want to take a taxi to this off-the-beaten-track location for the excellent traditional Mexican cuisine of chef Carmen Titita, author of several cookbooks, and a big name in the Mexico City culinary scene. Very popular with large families, especially on weekends, the food is traditional and there are always interesting choices: try the duck in black mole and the chongos for dessert, weirdly wonderful curdled milk dish.

As of 2006, a second branch of El Bajio opened at Parque Delta, a sleek shopping center at the corner of Cuauhtemoc and Viaducto, near the Centro Medico metro stop on the no. 1 or no. 3 lines), which is more accessible to the Centro, but lacks the ambience of the original. (both are only open for comida)

CENA (Dinner). The evening meal is usually a simple affair in most Mexican homes, but "going out for dinner" is becoming more a part of Mexico City

nightlife. Many of the places already mentioned are open for dinner as well, but here are a few places especially nice in the evening. Options for dining out in the Centro are limited at night; more restaurants are found in Polanco and Condesa.

Cafe Blanca (Cinco de Mayo 40), is one of the last of the old-time 1940's style coffe shops with a large menu of Mexican standards. Its counter service makes it a comfortable place for a single travelers. Open from 7am to 11pm.

Cafe Tacuba (Calle Tacuba 28, Centro). This landmark institution (since 1912) offers a veritable encyclopedia of classic Mexican dishes (enchiladas, sopes, chalupas, chiles rellenos) in a beautifully tiled colonial-style interior. There is often live music, and a festive Mexican atmosphere. Open for breakfast, lunch or dinner, it is a fun night out in the Centro, and is a traditional after-theater spot.

Fonda El Refugio (Liverpool 166, Zona Rosa, tel. 5525-8128) For more than 50 years this restaurant has set high standards for Mexican classics such as Chiles en nogada. It is a bit touristy, but still good.

ALTA COCINA MEXICANA

The concept of "high Mexican cuisine" is relatively new. Mexicans used to think (and many still do) that a fancy night out meant French food. Authors Diana Kennedy and Rick Bayless have brought awareness of Mexican cuisine to the U.S. through their books and TV shows. In Mexico a number of star chefs, most of them women, have changed attitudes toward local foods, once considered too humble to be taken seriously as cuisine. Here are a few of my favorite places, good for lunch or a fancy dinner. Reservations are recommended for all of these places. Expect to spend around US$40 to $60 per person. Waiters will gladly call you a taxi for your ride home.

Izote (513 Mazaryk, Polanco, 5280-1671). Owner/Chef/Author Patricia Quintana has created a smartly hip place with great food and comfortable ambience. Dishes such as lasagne de huitlacoche (made with a black corn fungus), or smoked salmon with avocado and vanilla are found on this intriguing menu (which comes in English, too). Be sure to check the daily specials, which tend to be … special. This is a good place to try ensalada de nopales or pozole. Desserts, especially the ones with chocolate and marzipan, are superb.

Taberna de León (Plaza Loreto, San Angel, tel. 5616-2110). Chef Mónica Patiño uses classic Mexican ingredients in new ways in this comfortably elegant restaurant, set in an old mansion in the Plaza Loreto Mall. The salads are remarkable for their flavorful organic greens.

Aguila y Sol (Moliere 42, Polanco (tel. 5281-8354). Marta Chapa is the third member of the culinary triumvirate (along with Quintana and Patiño) of important female chefs in Mexico City. This has perhaps the most creative menu of the group, with items such as ceviche with coconut and a salad of watermelon and queso panela. The decor is austere but elegant, the food and service impeccable.

Paxia (Avenida de la Paz 47, San Angel, tel. 5550-8355, www. paxia.com.mx) is a relative newcomer on the scene, with updated Mexican classics from various regions of Mexico. The pozole de mariscos is a winner.

Restaurante Pujol, (Francisco Petrarca 254, Polanco, 5545-4111, www.pujol.com.mx), has received international attention recently. Enrique Olvera offers an individualistic and insightful approach to Mexican cuisine.

STREET STALL AND MARKET FOOD

Some of the most delicious food in Mexico City is found in street stalls and markets. There are also some very scary looking cauldrons of viscera floating in dark red sauces that could turn you into a vegetarian quickly. It took me several years to work up the courage to start eating food from street stalls because I assumed that all of it was greasy and loaded with bacteria. While there is no guarantee of germ-free food—even in fancy restaurants—I follow some basic guidelines when choosing where to eat.

Check out the stall, and the cook, for cleanliness. If it doesn't look clean, forget it. I choose food that I can see being cooked, and avoid anything that looks too greasy. I avoid food cooked in deep fat, unless I can see that the oil is clean and very hot, which it rarely is. I don't eat food that looks like it has been sitting outside for a long time. I look for crowded stalls that have been discovered by locals–they have already selected the good

ones. Some vendors slip on a plastic glove before accepting money—a good sign. Make sure your hands are clean before you eat. I carry a package of moist towelettes with me. I avoid street food during hot weather.

Suggestions for street food are in all the Walking Tours, and good food stalls are also found clustered around many metro stations. One of the best is Chilpancingo (#9 train, near to Colonia Condesa). Outside the metro entrance along Calle Chilpancingo is a gauntlet of food vendors selling tacos, tlacoyos and quesadillas. The flautas and caldo de pollo near the corner are especially good.

MORE FOOD TIPS

Restaurante Chon (Regina 160, Centro, 5542-0873 www.restaurantechon.com). If you are curious about what the Aztecs ate, here's the place. This institution in the Centro offers prehispanic cuisine; ant eggs, grasshoppers, armadillo, and snake are among the rarities you will find here. The decor is like an Albanian airport lounge. Lunch only.

Mercado San Juan (Ernesto Pugibet, Centro). This is the market where professional chefs and serious cooks shop for the highest quality meat, fish, cheese, sausage and produce in the city, as well as imported goods: there are even a couple of Asian food stands. Sample the empanadas de elote (with corn and cheese) being sold from a basket out front by a venerable Argentine gentleman. For the adventurous, there are gusanos here, too (worms found in maguey cactus), which are eaten live, rolled up in a tortilla. Stall no. 283 does an excellent pozole on Saturdays.

Café Jekemir (Isabel la Católica near Regina, Centro). Forget those ubiquitous Seattle-based chains: I make a trip to the Centro to buy my Veracruzano coffee beans—they are the best as well as the cheapest. You can also sit and have a cup. It's easy to find—just follow the smell of roasted coffee. Owned and run by several genrations of a Lebanese family, it has become a hangout for classical musicians. Across the street is the restaurant Coox Hanal (p.90).

Mikasa (San Luis Potosí near Monterey, Colonia Roma). This market serves the Japanese community in Mexico City; there is excellent take-out food. You can buy lunch and walk over to nearby Parque Mexico in Condesa for a picnic lunch. On weekends there is an outdoor Japanese barbeque.

Mosaico (Michoacán near Insurgentes, Condesa). This fashionable bistro has a take-out charcuterie section with great sun-dried tomatoes, herring in curry sauce and ensalada de alubias (white bean salad) among other treats—another place to stock up for a picnic in nearby Parque Mexico.

La Naval (at the corner of Michoacán and Insurgentes, Condesa). Also near Parque Mexico is one of the best wine and liquor stores in the city, with a good bakery and deli counter as well.

La Europea (Lopez 60 and Ayuntamiento 25, Centro). A chain store with good selections of wines and tequilas

---

If you are a Mexican food aficionado, try to find a copy of the excellent *Diccionario Enciclopédico de Gastromomía Mexicana* by Ricardo Muñoz Zurita—it explains just about anything you can think of about Mexican food, ingredients and history (in Spanish only). Look in Ghandi or Casa Lamm bookstores.

THE TASTES OF MEXICO CITY

MY TOP TEN

WHEN YOU CAN'T STAND ANY MORE MEXICAN FOOD

Ehden (Gante 11-A, Centro) Good Middle Eastern food is served at outdoor tables on this pedestrian-only street.

Centro Castellano (Uruguay 16, Centro) You will find classic Spanish food and inviting atmosphere here.

Daikoku (Michoacán 25, Condesa, tel. 5584-9419). Reliable Japanese food, good sushi, but ugly decor. I avoid the chain restaurants such as Sushi Itto, which you will see around town—even the rice was bad. At almost all Japanese restaurants you will notice the phenomenon of cream cheese added to sushi— a curious Mexican innovation I have not adapted to. If you don't want queso crema, let them know when you order. It is one of the few places that stay open for dinner on Sunday.

Hotel Nikko (Campos Eliseos 204, Polanco, tel. 5281-6828). There is a pan-Asian buffet daily at the Restaurant O'Mei and an excellent Japanese buffet (Sunday comida only) at the Restaurant Benkay. A bargain at around US$20.

MP Bistro (Andres Bello 10, Polanco, tel. 5280-2506). Mónica Patiño (see p.92) has created a fusion of Mexican, French and Asian cuisines that draws an upscale crowd. Her new **Delirio**, at Monterrey 116 in Roma looks promising.

Vucciria (Avenida Mexico 157, Condesa, 5564-7441) Italian food is served at this attractive restaurant overlooking Parque Mexico, also open late on Sunday.

Photo Bistro (Amsterdam at Plaza Citlatepetl, Condesa). Owned by a French photographer, this hip but comfortable spot has good bistro classics (excellent onion soup) and changing photo exhibitions.

Mosaico (Michoacán between Insurgentes and Amsterdam), Tasty French and Spanish bistro food and great people watching are the highlights here.

Agapi Mu (Alfonso Reyes 96, Condesa, 5286-1384). Good Greek food is served in a cool and pleasant setting, like being in a whitewashed Greek house.

El Dragón (Hamburgo 97, Zona Rosa, tel. 5525-2466). This is red-lantern kind of Chinese place that is pleasing and reliable.

Tezka (Amberes 78, Zona Rosa, tel. 5228-9918) The menu at this famous Basque restaurant is the creation of world-renowned chef Juan Mari Arzak of Spain. The tasting menu is a good deal at under US$50 per person, but the decor looks like a fancy retirement home.

BEST BARS AND CANTINAS

Bar la Opera (Cinco de Mayo 10, Centro) This landmark bar is classic and comforting. See Walking Tour of Centro p.21

La Terraza del Zócalo (Plaza de la Constitución 13, 6th floor). Don't let the entry and elevator put you off—this clean and attractive place has the best views of the Zócalo.

El Nivel (Moneda 1, Centro) The oldest cantina in the city (1855) is just off the Zócalo. See Walking Tour of Centro #3.

Blue Lounge (Hotel Camino Real, Mariano Escobedo 700, Anzures). This bar, with a glass floor over a shallow pool, is the place for high heels and slinky black dresses.

La Bodega (Avenida Popocatépetl 25 at Avenida Amsterdam, Condesa, 5525-2473). Good live Afro-Cuban music, and a homey atmosphere that feels like Greenwich Village in the 60's, keep this place ever popular. There is a small theater upstairs featuring local cabaret artists. Closed Sundays.

Condesa DF (Veracruz at Parque España, Condesa). The rooftop bar at this trendy and chic hotel is a great place at sunset or later.

El Tio Pepe (at the corner of Independencia and Dolores, Centro) This 1870 cantina preserves its funky charm under decades of paint. It's a good place for a drink before going to Bellas Artes.

WHAT TO DO AT NIGHT

Check listings in Tiempo Libre or Chilango magazines for current events of dance, theater or music.

Attend a performance at the **Palacio de Bellas Artes** if you can. The theatre itself is a work of art. The colorful Ballet Folklórico performs every Wednesday and Sunday night at 8:30 as well as Sunday mornings at 9:30.

Plaza Garibaldi (Eje Central and Honduras, Centro) is the place to go for authentic mariachi music. Mariachis are the guys you see in the tight-fitting suits decorated with metal studs and embroidery, and wearing wide sombreros. The image and the sound are associated with Mexico worldwide. Mariachis perform at birthday parties, weddings and political rallies; they are the ultimate expression of joyful national pride. Groups usually include guitars, violins and trumpets. At Plaza Garibaldi musical mayhem reigns as people hire musicians to play their favorite songs, with many groups play at once. It is a unique sonic experience. There are bars and restaurants surrounding the area (some of which can be surprisingly expensive, so check prices before you order), but just strolling around the plaza is a quintessential Mexico City experience. Be careful with your wallets and pocketbooks here. There is a taxi sitio right out front.

Zinco (Motolinia 20, near Cinco de Mayo, Centro, tel. 5512-3369) This late night club (opens 10PM) in the cellar of an Art-Deco building features the best jazz musicians in town. Price varies according to event. Papa Beto Jazz Bistro Villalongín 196-H, near Circuito Interior, Col. Cuauhtémoc, tel. 5592-1632)

El Gran León (Querétaro 225, between Monterrey and Medellin in Colonia Roma) A "Little Cuba" section of the city has sprung up with several bars, restaurants and dance clubs. Our favorite is El Nuevo León, a big old-fashioned dance hall with great live music and an easy-going crowd. There is no problem if you don't bring a dance partner, or even if you don't dance well—everybody ends up having a good time. Lively Mamá Rumba down the street appeals to singles and young couples. Open Thursday through Saturday from 9:30PM to 3:30AM. The doorman can get you a safe cab home.

La Bodega (Calle Amsterdam at Popocatepetl in Colonia

Condesa—closed Sundays). You can eat, drink, listen to live Cuban music, and dance at this comfortable and unpretentious place. There is also a small theater upstairs with performers such as the eccentric songstress Astrid Hadad, known as "the Mexican Bette Midler." (check her out at www.astridhadad.com).

Living Reforma, Reforma 483, near El Angel, tel. 5286-0069, is the current mixed (gay/straight) trendy disco. Open Friday and Saturday from 10 on.

La Casa de Paquita la del Barrio (Zarco 202, Centro, tel. 5583-8131) Paquita is a singer of enormous popularity in Mexico with her own club in the working class Guerrero section of the Centro. A big, tough-looking woman who rarely smiles, Paquita sings about women in a way reminiscent of Bessie Smith. Her most famous song "Tres Veces" has the refrain "I cheated on you three times—the first time in rage, the second time on a whim, the third time for pleasure." Call to make sure she's not on tour.

Inauguraciones Go to an art opening. Look in Tiempo Libre magazine under the Museos y Galerias section, where there are special listings for Inauguraciones (Openings). Galleries listed in the Polanco, Condesa and Roma sections of this book, as well as any of the major museums, will be likely to have fun and interesting openings. There is also a good listing on the website www.arte-mexico.com.

Cinema Mexico City is a great movie town. There are numerous annual film festivals—keep an eye out for posters at bus stops. Weekly listings are found in Tiempo Libre magazine, but they are arranged by theater chain, so it helps to know which theaters are near you. In the Centro look for listings under Cinemex Palacio Chino, Cinemex Real Cinema, Cinepolis Diana and Lumiere Reforma. In Colonia Condesa, it´s the Cinemex Plaza Insurgentes or Cinemex WTC, Colonia Roma has the Cinemex Cuauhtémoc, and in Polanco, look for the Cinemex Casa de Arte.

The **Cineteca Nacional** at the northern edge of Coyoacán (Avenida Mexico-Coyoacan 389, near Rio Churubusco—take a taxi or walk from Metro Coyoacán) shows an interesting mix of international films, new and old in a 7-theater complex with boosktore and café.

Some theaters of the Cinepolis chain offer VIP salons, where you can relax in wide reclining chairs as waiters serve sushi—the tickets cost twice as much (around 90 pesos) but it's worth it.

GAY NIGHT LIFE

Gay travelers will generally find Mexico a comfortable place to visit. Mexicans are tolerant and apparently easy-going about sexuality, in spite of the force of the Catholic Church. Mexican culture is slowly recognizing its own sexual diversity, but within families a policy of "don't ask, don't tell" often prevails. Still, it is not unheard of to see same-sex couples walking hand-in-hand or even kissing in public.

Tiempo Libre has listings of bars and discos (constantly changing) but there are a few old standbys that are always entertaining. In the Zona Rosa gay life centers around Calle Amberes near Reforma with several bars, restaurants and stores, generally catering to an under-30 crowd. Living Reforma (see p. 99), El Taller, Lipstick and Cabaret-Tito are among the most popular night spots here.

In the Centro, **El oasis** and **Viena** (Republica de Cuba near Eje Central) are working class cantinas with friendly ambience and neonlight decor. On weekends there is a floor show that might even include a gay mariachi or waiters doing a striptease. If you are looking for a gay experience that is truly Mexican, this is it.

Tom's Leather Bar (Insurgentes 357 near Michoacán, La Condesa), is a very popular bar for middle class gay men over 30. It has beautiful, uninhibited go-go boys after 11pm. Closed Mondays.

Amsterdam 219, Amsterdam 219, Condesa, Mexico City Mod lounge and bar draws a youngish mixed crowd. Good for a drink before a night on the town.

There are fewer choices for gay women in Mexico City—some bars have a special night for lesbians. Check weekly listings in Tiempo Libre magazine and also the website www.eventoslesbicos.org.

El Armorio Abierto (Augustin Melgar near Pachuca, Condesa, www.elarmarioabierto.com) is a bookstore that specializes in gay themes, mostly in Spanish.

www.sergay.com.mx will fill you in on any other information about the GLBT community you may need.

A Fountain in Colonia Roma

WHERE TO SHOP

Sanborn's This chain of stores is mentioned throughout the book, and you will see them all over Mexico. It is very handy for books, magazine, pharmacy items, chocolate, and a light meal. You can always find clean bathrooms and an ATM. Some are open all night.

Fonart (Juarez 89, Centro and also Patriotismo 691, Mixcoac) The Fundación Nacional de Artesanias is a chain of stores throughout the country selling craftwork from all regions of Mexico. There is a good selection of ceramics, glass, weaving, basketry, woodwork and more at reasonable prices. Once a year, usually beginning in October, there is a national craft exposition at the Juarez branch–that's where you will find the very best work. (www.fonart.gob.mx)

Victor (Madero #10) is a old store with an appealing selection of Mexican handicrafts and silver jewelry. It`s a bit hidden—you must walk through a perfume store and go upstairs to find it, but it's worth it. If you are a serious shopper, ask to see the other locked rooms.

Museo de Arte Popular (Independencia and Revillagigedo, Centro). The gift store at this excellent museum has a good selection of crafts at reasonable prices. All profits go to the artisans.

Artesanìas Monte de Piedad 11, opposite the Palacio Nacional on the Zócalo. You will find several floors of good quality Mexican crafts here, as well as a restaurant on the top floor with great views.

La Ciudadela (Balderas at Emilio Donde, Centro). This market has dozens of stalls selling traditional handmade items at good prices. You will find hammocks, glassware, baskets, sombreros, textiles, silver and lots more good things to bring home. It is the best of the various tourist markets around town. On Saturday afternoons there is outdoor dancing at the Plaza de Danzón nearby (see p.36).

Palacio de Máscaras (Allende 84, between Honduras and Ecuador, Centro), has more than 5000 masks (mostly new) from all parts of Mexico.

La Lagunilla (along Reforma at Jaime Nuno near metro Garibaldi, Sundays only). This is the best flea market in town and there are prizes to be had if you know how to bargain. You will find old Mexican pottery, hand-forged hardware, antique furniture, jewelry, Nazi memorabilia, books, cd's—a bit of everything. Look for vendors selling horchata de coco (a delicious coconut drink) and tacos de bacalao for a snack as you shop. There are also good quesadilla and tlacoyo vendors here.

New books Ghandi is the largest bookseller with two locations. One is directly across from the Palacio de Bellas Artes (which also has its own good bookstore). The largest Ghandi is located at Miguel Angel de Quevedo no.128 near Avenida Universidad in Coyoacan. Casa Lamm in Colonia Roma also has a good bookstore with large selection of travel and art books. Centro Cultural Bella Época, (Tamaulipas 202 at Benjamin Hill) is a large, well-stocked bookstore, gallery, café, cinema, and children's play area housed in a smartly renovated Art Deco movie theater in Colonia Condesa.

Used books Two areas specialize in used books of all

kinds. In the Centro along Calle Donceles, and in Colonia Roma along Alvaro Obregon (near Casa Lamm.)

La Europea This chain of stores has the best selection of wines and tequilas in town. Locations in the Centro at Ayuntamiento 21 and Lopez 60.

Upscale shopping Avenida President Masaryk in Polanco is where you will find the line-up of big name stores—Bulgari, Gucci, Fendi, etc. The nearby Centro Commercial Moliere is a very elegant shopping center. The slick Santa Fe Mall on the far western edge of the city is the largest in Latin America. Two department store chains, Palacio de Hierro and Liverpool, have branches throughout the city; prices tend to be high as many items are imported.

A BRIEF HISTORY OF MEXICAN ART, ARCHITECTURE AND CRAFTS

PRE-HISPANIC ART

The most important art in Mexico before the conquest was made by the Olmecs on the Gulf coast (1200 B.C. to 1 A.D.), the Mayas in the Yucatan (300 to 900A.D.), and the Aztecs in the valley of Mexico (1350 to 1521 A.D.), when the Spanish came and trashed the place. The culture of Teotihuacán (100 to 700 A.D.), whose ruins lie 50km northeast of the city, stands apart as a major influence on subsequent art, but not a direct ethnic lineage. The best places to see this art are the Museo de Antropología, The Museo del Templo Mayor, the Museo Dolores Olmedo, and the Museo Anahuacalli.

COLONIAL ART

Mexico was a colony of Spain until 1821, and influences of art of this period are mainly European in style and religious in content. Miguel Cabrera and Juan Correa are artists from the 1700's whose work stands out. The best places to see Colonial Art are the Museo Nacional, the Museo del Carmen, the Museo Franz Mayer, and the Museo San Carlos.

POST-INDEPENDENCE ART

Although European influence still dominated the scene, self awareness in Mexican art began to emerge in the 19th century. The native land-scapes of José Maria Velasco (1840–1912 are evocative and proud. The popular black and white prints of José Guadalupe Posada (1852–1913) used caricature and political satire as their tools, and his skeletal images have become Mexican icons. The artist known as Dr. Atl (1875–1964) painted landscapes (he was especially fond of volcanos) noted for their intense, emotional color. See this art at the Museo Nacional.

THE MURALIST MOVEMENT

When things settled down after the 1910 Revolution, the government began a program of public mural painting to encourage awareness of Mexican heritage. Its most famous is Diego Rivera (1885–1957), per-haps better know now as the husband of artist.Frida Kahlo. The two other most important muralists are José Clement Orozco (1883–1949) and David Alfaro Siqueiros (1896–1974), whose works tend to have a more strident political feel. Juan O'Gorman (also a noted architect) designed massive mosaic murals at the University. Rufino Tamayo is another important artist of this period who painted murals.

There are murals all over town, but some of the best places to visit are the Palacio Nacional, the Secretaria de Educación Publica and the Museo Mural Diego Rivera (these 3 have the best of Rivera); The Palacio de Bellas Artes and the Castillo de Chapultepec have murals by several artists.

FRIDA KAHLO
One tires quickly of the images slapped on t-shirts and shopping bags, but the almost-naive art of this doomed heroine retains its haunting power when you see it in person. The best collection is at the Museo Dolores Olmedo. The Museo de Arte Moderno owns a few important works, but Frida's own house has mostly sketches and lesser works.

CONTEMPORARY MEXICAN ART
Much of what one sees in Mexico City art galleries looks an imitation of New York or Berlin, trying hard to be cool, looking like too much time was spent in art school; however, a few younger artists have made names for themselves in the world art market.Gabriel Orozco stands out with his quirky sculptures and installations. In Oaxaca, a rich art scene has develpoed in the last 10 years, headed by Francisco Toledo; these artists incorporate indigineous elements into their work.

PRE-HISPANIC ARCHITECTURE

The scale model of Aztec Mexico City in the Museo de Antropología offers a teasing idea of the the architecture, as do the ruins at the Templo Mayor—use your imagination here. Teotihuacán is the best place to see near-complete examples of pre-Hispanic architecture on the grandest scale.

COLONIAL ARCHITECTURE

European grandeur arrived with the Spaniards, whose architectural legacy is strong in Mexico City. Flamboyant Baroque highlights include the main altar of the Catedral, the Palacio de Iturbide, and the Santo Domingo church in the Centro. The best ensemble of neo-classic architecture surrounds the Plaza Manuel Tolsá by the Museo Nacional.

PORFIRIATO ARCHITECTURE

The reign of President Porfírio Díaz (1876 to 1910) lasted long enough to claim its own architectural style. He left the stamp of Paris all over the country; the cast-iron bandstands one sees in towns all over Mexico date from this period. The finest architectural examples are the exterior of the Palacio de Bellas Artes, the Correo Mayor, and the residential architecture of Colonia Roma.

ART DECO

Aztec influence on Deco design of the 1920's and 1930's give it a unique flavor in Mexico. The interior of the Palacio de Bellas Artes is the supreme example of this style, and Colonia Condesa is one of the best-preserved Art Deco neighborhoods in the world.

CONTEMPORARY ARCHITECTURE

Luis Barragan is the most important name in 20th century Mexican architecture. You can visit his home and studio. Ricardo Legorreta is a disciple of Barragan's whose most recent work is a group of graceful government buildings along the Alameda. The Museo de Antropología by Pedro Ramírez Vásquez

Art Nouveau house in La Roma

from the 1960's uses pre-Hispanic references with International style. Examples of daring designs of high-rise commercial buildings can be seen along Reforma, Insurgentes Sur, and in the Santa Fe area at the western end of the city, which looks a bit like Tokyo. The Centro Nacional de las Artes is a showcase for architecture by 20th century Mexican masters.

CRAFTS

Mexican artisans are famous world wide as potters, weavers, jewelers, wood carvers, mask makers, and metal workers. Spanish priests advanced the cause of Mexican craftsmanship by organizing indigenous guilds and encouraging trade, and the government continues its support. In many places, the quality of crafts has fallen with the influence of mass-produced items, but good things are still being made. The finest craft regions are in the states of Oaxaca and Michoacán. The Museo de Arte Popular has the best collection in town, and a good gift store, too. FONART stores, Artesanias on the Zócalo, and the Ciudadela market are the best places in Mexico City to shop for crafts.

MEXICAN MUSIC

La Llorona, Oil on Canvas, by Nicholas Gilman

Traditional Mexican music has deep roots in indigenous music, European popular song, flamenco, and German music. While current global trends are what you will often hear in the street, tradition dies hard and many performers keep the flame burning: even teenagers know the old songs.

Ranchera, or country music, encompasses Folk, Mariachi, *Norteña, banda, Jarocho* and a host of other idioms. The era of "Great Divas and Divos" of Ranchera is past (think Sinatra and Clooney) but their recordings are widely available. **Lola Beltran**, *"La Reina de la Canción Ranchera"* sang definitive versions of classic rancheras; when she died, people from all walks of life lined up for blocks to see her layed out in state in Bellas Artes. Runner up was **Amalia Mendoza**, whose best known hit was *Amarga Navidad*, or "Bitter Christmas, which ends with lots of melodramatic weeping and wailing. Other great voices were **Lucha Villa, Yolanda Del Rio** and **Rócio Durcal**. Octagenerian **Chavela Vargas** has at last received her due fame, thanks to some promotion by Pedro Almodóvar, and she has become a willing lesbian icon.

Pop singer **Ana Gabriel**, with a distinctive gravelly voice, has a wonderful album of traditional music, *Joyas de Dos Siglos*, accompanying herself on guitar. **Linda Ronstadt** has made a big impression with her versions of classic songs on three albums, all good, and she pays tribute to the greats who preceded her. The original, "Mexican Piaf" was **Lucha Reyes**, the first woman to record Ranchera music.

The great male singers of the genre are **Pedro Vargas, Javier Solis** and **Jose Alfredo Jimenez**, also a beloved composer. **Pedro Infante** and **Jorge Negrete** are golden-voiced crooners who were also big matinee idols of the 1940's. **Alejandro Fernandez**, who has become even more famous than his father Vicente, is a current heartthrob with a beautiful voice.

Bolero, or "Ballad" music is a style closer to classic American pop, *Besame Mucho* being the most well known example of a Bolero. Songwriter and performer *"el músico-poeta"* Agustín Lara wrote thousands of songs, including *Granada,* that are still known and sung. His muse, **Toña la Negra**, was the best interpreter of his music (Ronstadt pays tribute to her). Her recordings from the '50's are the best. Nobody in Mexico seems to know that **Eydie Gormé**, who recorded a pair of wonderful albums with the **Trio los Panchos** in the '60's, is a gringa, so flawless is her accent. Today, **Eugenia León** who possesses an extraordinary, large, voice, has inhereted the mantel of Queen Diva in just about every genre; her *Tirana* album is the best. Opera stars **Olivia Gorra** and **Fernando de la Mora** have also done good albums of boleros: look for her *Pecadora* and his *Boleros*.

The L.A. based group **Los Lobos** recorded an exemplary album of folk music, *La Pistola y el Corazón.* **Amparo Ochoa** was a chronicler of traditional folk songs and *corridas*, songs that tell stories. Several younger singers have revived interest in more traditional folk styles: **Lila Downs, Georgina Meneses** and **Susana Harp**.

There is a rich body of Mexican "classical" music, from localized European styles of the colonial era, to distinguished modern composers of the 20th century such as Silvestre Revueltas, Carlos Chavez and Manuel M. Ponce who incorporated elements of folk styles into their work.

Mexican Cinema

Since the late 1930's, when Spain and Argentina stopped making much cinema due to political strife, Mexico has been the leading center of Spanish language film (and later television). The industry's "Golden Age" was the 1940's and '50's, when many films were made either in genres similar to those of Hollywood, or styles peculiar to Mexico, such as the *Ranchera* and *Rumbera* films. While free trade allowed Hollywood to flood the market and nearly extinguish film production here, since the early '90's, some excellent independent films dealing with urban Chilango life have been drawing new attention to "Frijoliwood": *Callejón de Los Milagros, Amores Perros, Y Tu Mamá También,* as well as such contemporary adult comedies as *Sexo Pudor y Lágrimas, Nicotina* and *Profundo Carmesi* stand out. Many of these are available in inexpensive DVD versions, some with English subtitles.

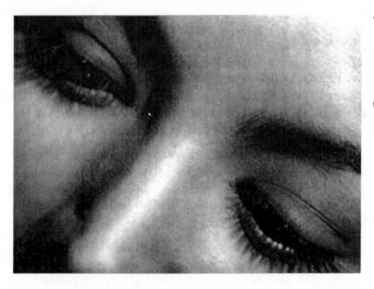

photo Gabriel Figueroa

1. Santa (1931)

The first sound film made in Mexico from the best-selling novel by Fernando Gamboa. Agustin Lara's song of the same name is sung to accompany an extraordinary brothel scene. It was filmed partly in Colonia Condesa, and was the first of a genre of "good girl gone bad" movies.

2. La Mujer del Puerto (1933)

Good girl becomes whore, through no fault of her own ... starring the fabulous Andrea Palma the "Mexican Dietrich".

3. Allá en el Rancho Grande (1936)

The archetypal Comedia Ranchera, a genre popular until the 1990's when Hollywood and free trade practically killed off the Mexican cinema industry.

4. Distinto Amanecer (Another Dawn) (1943)

One of the greatest film noirs ever made, rivaling Casablanca—once again starring Andrea Palma and making Pedro Armendariz a star. The train station finale gives one goose bumps!

5. Maria Candelaria (1943)

The first product of the great team of director Emilio "El Indio" Fernandez and cinematographer Gabriel Figueroa, and Dolores Del Rio's return to Mexican Cinema after a long stay in Hollywood. Made in conjunction with intellectuals and artists (including Diego Rivera) to promote the nobility of Mexican indigenous culture. Filmed on location in the "floating gardens of Xochimilco" (where everyone can tell you, to this day, which canals were used as locations).

6. Enamorada (1946)

Maria Felix was Latin America's greatest star, not well known in the USA as she never worked in Hollywood. This is her best film, another Fernandez/Figueroa collaboration, and a prototype of the Revolutionary film genre. The scene where Felix is serenaded and the camera zooms up to her eye is justly famous.

7. **Salón México** (1946)
Another Fernandez/Figueroa collaboration, and a noir classic, which made the late Marga Lopez a star. Another suffering-taxi dancer (read:prostitute) story, beautifully filmed and all taking place in Mexico City at night (in the rain, naturally).

8. **Los Olvidados** (1950). Filmed on locations in Mexico City (including Colonia Roma and the Centro), Luis Buñuel's superb portrait of the struggling classes was banned shortly after its premier, offending some for showing Mexico in a bad light. In 2005 it was the first film to be named by UNESCO as part of their Universal Cultural Patrimony program.

9. **Nosotros los Pobres** (1948) Starring the great singer/actor Pedro Infante who created the archetype Pepe el Toro, the urban working class hero. It was an attempt to depict and dignify the working class poor of Mexico City, several years before the more sophisticated (and pessimistic) Los Ovidados was made. This is the best known and beloved film in all of Mexican cinema, like "It's A Wonderful Life" is in the USA.

10. **Aventurera** (1949) The best known in a series of lurid Rumbera films, another genre peculiar to Mexican Cinema which combines noir and musical numbers, and usually takes place in the underworld of nightclubs and gangsters. It stars Cuban actress Ninón Sevilla.

RECOMMENDED READING

1. **History of the Conquest of New Spain** by Bernal Díaz del Castillo—an amazing description of Tenochtitlàn by one of Cortez' followers.

2. **Life in Mexico** by Frances Calderon De La Barca—Life in New Spain in the early 19th century.

3. **Sor Juana's Love Poems** by Sor Juana Inez de la Cruz. Mexico's great 17th century poet is well translated in this short collection, presented in both Spanish and English..

4. **The Underdogs** by Mariano Azuela. Mexico's first novel of the revolution.

5. **Pedro Páramo** by Juan Rulfo who had a major influence in the development of magical realism.

6. **Where the Air is Clear** by Carlos Fuentes is a modern urban epic by Mexico's best known contemporary novelist.

7. **The Labyrinth of Solitude** by Octavio Paz will give you an insight into the Mexican national character.

8. **La Capital: the Biography of Mexico City** by Jonathan Kandell is a fun and informative read.

9. **Frida: A Biography of Frida Kahlo** by Hayden Herrera Even if you haven't been caught up by "Frida-mania", this bio is worth reading as it paints a vivid portrait of the Golden Age of Mexican culture of the 1920's-1950's.

10. Englishman B.Traven wrote about Mexico like an insider. If you can read Spanish, his **Canasta de Cuentos Mexicanos** is superb, and funny as hell.

INDEX

photo: Nicholas Gilman

ABOUT THE AUTHOR

Jim Johnston was born in New York City and grew up in the woods of New Hampshire. After studying architecture at the University of Virginia and graphic design at the School of Visual Arts, he worked as a professional artist and potter in New York City for many years before moving full-time to Mexico in 1996, where he continues working as a printmaker. He currently resides in Mexico City with his partner Nicholas Gilman.

WWW.JIMJOHNSTONART.COM

978-0-595-41841-1
0-595-41841-4

Printed in the United States
92613LV00002BA/16-24/A